D1489671

TONY EVANS
KINGDOM MAN
— DEVOTIONAL —

DAILY INSPIRATION FOR
FULFILLING YOUR DESTINY

FOCUS
ON THE FAMILY

TYNDALE HOUSE PUBLISHERS
CAROL STREAM, ILLINOIS

KINGDOM MAN DEVOTIONAL
Copyright © 2013 Focus on the Family

A Focus on the Family book published by
Tyndale House Publishers, Carol Stream, Illinois 60188

Focus on the Family and the accompanying logo and design are federally registered
trademarks of Focus on the Family, Colorado Springs, CO 80995.

TYNDALE, Tyndale's quill logo, and *LeatherLike* are registered trademarks of Tyndale
House Ministries.

Scripture quotations, unless otherwise marked, are taken from the *New American
Standard Bible*®. Copyright © 1960, 1962, 1963, 1968, 1971, 1972, 1973, 1975,
1977, 1995 by The Lockman Foundation. Used by permission. (www.Lockman.org).

Scripture quotations marked ESV are taken from *The Holy Bible, English Standard
Version*®, (ESV®). Copyright © 2001 by Crossway, a publishing ministry of Good
News Publishers. Used by permission. All rights reserved.

Scripture quotations marked HCSB have been taken from the *Holman Christian
Standard Bible*®. Copyright © 1999, 2000, 2002, 2003, 2009 by Holman Bible
Publishers. Used by permission. Holman Christian Standard Bible®, Holman CSB®,
and HCSB® are federally registered trademarks of Holman Bible Publishers. All rights
reserved.

Scripture quotations marked KJV are taken from the *Holy Bible, King James Version*.

All Scripture quotations marked NIV are taken from the *Holy Bible, New International
Version*®. NIV®. Copyright © 1973, 1978, 1984 by Biblica, Inc.™ Used by permission
of Zondervan. All rights reserved worldwide (www.zondervan.com).

Scripture quotations marked MSG are taken from *The Message* [paraphrase]. Copyright
© by Eugene H. Peterson 1993, 1994, 1995, 1996, 2000, 2001, 2002. Used by
permission of NavPress Publishing Group.

Editorial contributors: Jeremy Jones, Jesse Florea, Bob Smithouser, and Marianne
Hering

Cover and wrap designs by Jennifer Ghionzoli
Photograph of man taken by Stephen Vosloo. Copyright © Focus on the Family.
All rights reserved.

Image of skyline copyright © Trigger Photo/iStock Photo. All rights reserved.

For information about special discounts for bulk purchases, please contact Tyndale
House Publishers at csresponse@tyndale.com, or call 1-800-323-9400.

ISBN 978-1-62405-121-0 (LeatherLike)
ISBN 978-1-58997-946-8 (Hardcover) (SPEC)

Printed in China

26   25   24   23   22   21   20
14   13   12   11   10   9   8

Contents

Introduction 1

1. A Kingdom Man Seeks Priceless Treasure 2
2. A Kingdom Man Aims for the Goal 4
3. A Kingdom Man 6
4. A Kingdom Man Follows His Rule Book 8
5. A Kingdom Man Is Prepared 10
6. A Kingdom Man Makes the Right Choice . . . 12
7. A Kingdom Man Brings Freedom 14
8. A Kingdom Man Builds a Legacy 16
9. A Kingdom Man Rules Under God's
   Authority 18
10. A Kingdom Man Takes Responsibility 20
11. A Kingdom Man Has Got It 22
12. A Kingdom Man Trusts that God's Got It 24
13. A Kingdom Man Longs to Be Great 26
14. A Kingdom Man Finds Strength
    in Meekness 28
15. A Kingdom Man Is Free to Pursue
    Greatness 30
16. A Kingdom Man Serves 32
17. A Kingdom Man Plays His Position 34
18. A Kingdom Man Stops Making Excuses 36

19. A Kingdom Man Advances One Step
    at a Time 38
20. A Kingdom Man Makes the Most
    of What He Has 40
21. A Kingdom Man Chooses to Be the One 42
22. A Kingdom Man Is Heroic 44
23. A Kingdom Man Rejects False Manhood 46
24. A Kingdom Man Realigns 48
25. A Kingdom Man Acts His Age 50
26. A Kingdom Man Owns Up Beyond
    the Bedroom........................ 52
27. A Kingdom Man Aligns His Attitude 54
28. A Kingdom Man Puts Women and
    Children First....................... 56
29. A Kingdom Man Is a Hero 58
30. A Kingdom Man Readies Himself
    for Judgment 60
31. A Kingdom Man Imitates Christ 62
32. A Kingdom Man Accepts His Role 64
33. A Kingdom Man Understands His
    Boundary 66
34. A Kingdom Man Brings Out the Sun 68
35. A Kingdom Man Is Consistent 70
36. A Kingdom Man Rejects a Double
    Standard........................... 72
37. A Kingdom Man Belongs to a Church 74

38. A Kingdom Man Is a Pastor 76
39. A Kingdom Man Roars 78
40. A Kingdom Man Finds Power in the Word . . . 80
41. A Kingdom Man Tends His Garden 82
42. A Kingdom Man Is a Delegate 84
43. A Kingdom Man Is Royal 86
44. A Kingdom Man Seeks God's Plan 88
45. A Kingdom Man Gathers Strength 90
46. A Kingdom Man Is Equipped 92
47. A Kingdom Man Chooses Yes 94
48. A Kingdom Man Sees with Perspective 96
49. A Kingdom Man Focuses on Victory 98
50. A Kingdom Man Matters 100
51. A Kingdom Man Is Free 102
52. A Kingdom Man Waits Actively 104
53. A Kingdom Man Obeys in Faith 106
54. A Kingdom Man Values His Help 108
55. A Kingdom Man Demonstrates Love 110
56. A Kingdom Man Blesses 112
57. A Kingdom Man Names God's Work 114
58. A Kingdom Man Has a Calling to Name 116
59. A Kingdom Man Knows True Success 118
60. A Kingdom Man Sees True Victory 120
61. A Kingdom Man Plays with Confidence 122
62. A Kingdom Man Prays from the Heart 124
63. A Kingdom Man Wrestles with God 126

64. A Kingdom Man Reaches into Heaven 128

65. A Kingdom Man Plugs Into Power 130

66. A Kingdom Man Leaves the Past Behind 132

67. A Kingdom Man Walks in Faith 134

68. A Kingdom Man Seizes His Inheritance 136

69. A Kingdom Man Defeats Giants 138

70. A Kingdom Man Follows God's Leading 140

71. A Kingdom Man Has a Vision 142

72. A Kingdom Man Prays 144

73. A Kingdom Man Is a Blessing 146

74. A Kingdom Man Fears the Lord 148

75. A Kingdom Man Gives God His Best 150

76. A Kingdom Man Denies Himself 152

77. A Kingdom Man Sharpens Others 154

78. A Kingdom Man Defends the Family 156

79. A Kingdom Man Doesn't Turn Back 158

80. A Kingdom Man Lays It All Down 160

81. A Kingdom Man Cherishes His Wife 162

82. A Kingdom Man Is Focused on the
Right Thing 164

83. A Kingdom Man Is Part of Something
Bigger Than Himself 166

84. A Kingdom Man Is an Example to His
Family 168

85. A Kingdom Man Is Rooted with Other
Believers 170

86. A Kingdom Man Lives His Faith
    Publicly.............................. 172
87. A Kingdom Man Makes an Impact 174
88. A Kingdom Man Loves Well 176
89. A Kingdom Man Strengthens Those
    in Need 178
90. A Kingdom Man Passes the Baton 180

Notes 183

Introduction

A kingdom man is a man who visibly demonstrates the comprehensive rule of God underneath the Lordship of Jesus Christ in every area of his life.
—Tony Evans, *Kingdom Man*

God has a work for you to do, noble work that is worthy of a kingdom man (Ephesians 2:10). To help prepare you for great things, each Kingdom Man devotion further develops a spiritual theme introduced by Dr. Tony Evans in the best-selling book *Kingdom Man*.

Come alongside Tony every day as he shares essential truths about male leadership and God's transforming power. The inspirational biblical principles in these pages will equip you to do good works in your home, church, and community.

A Kingdom Man Seeks Priceless Treasure

*The kingdom of heaven is like
a treasure hidden in the field . . .*
—Jesus (Matthew 13:44)

One of my favorite Indiana Jones movies is about the search for the Holy Grail. In the movie's climactic moment, the famed archaeologist is in the Grail chamber with an ancient guardian knight. Indy stands in the candlelit room, looking at the shelves filled with dozens of cups and chalices. One of the goblets is the legendary Holy Grail, the cup of Christ said to possess ultimate power. Jones must select the right one or he and his father will die.

"You must choose, but choose wisely," says the guardian knight. "For while the true Grail will bring you life, the false Grail will take it from you."[1]

Even if you've never seen *Indiana Jones and the Last Crusade*, you know what happens: Indy always uncovers the treasure.[2]

Men, you have a choice. Jesus speaks of a treasure: "The kingdom of heaven is like a treasure hidden in a field," He said (Matthew 13:44). It's a treasure for which absolutely nothing should stand in the way. In eschatological terms, the kingdom refers to the millennial reign of Christ when He will return to run earth from Jerusalem for His thousand-year reign. Yet in the here and now, the kingdom has also been set up for us through kingdom principles, covenants, responsibilities, privileges, rights, rules, ethics, coverings, and authority. This is a priceless treasure, one worth everything you have. Choose wisely.

APPLICATION

1. Who is your favorite movie character? What about him inspires you?

2. How would your current life play out on the big screen?

3. What treasure will you fight for today? How?

PRAYER

God, give me a vision of Your kingdom and the strength to pursue it like a treasure hunter. Amen.

2

A Kingdom Man
Aims for the Goal

My son Jonathan is a big guy who has played in the NFL. When he was young and five-foot-three, he asked me to come to the gym and watch him dunk the basketball. He had been practicing for months. Jonathan dribbled and dunked. I offered abbreviated congratulations. Then I turned to the athletic director and pointedly told him to raise the basket back up to where it belonged. Impatient to grow taller, Jonathan had lowered the goal.

Men, God has a standard. He has a goal. His kingdom is that goal. Yet so many have lowered His standard only to congratulate themselves for being able to dunk the ball. The results of this lowered standard, though, affect us all. It shows up in our country. In our culture. In the economics of our world. It takes only a cursory glance around our homes, churches, communities, and globe to uncover that many men have missed the goal to live as kingdom men.

That must change.

The apostle Paul said, "Do you not know that those who run in a race all run, but only one receives the prize? Run in such a way that you may win" (1 Corinthians 9:24). We must run to win. We must raise the standard to where God originally placed it. We must define manhood as God intended it to be.

Application

1. In what areas of your life have you lowered the goal?

2. Are there any pursuits or possessions that have distracted you from the standard of God's kingdom?

3. What scripture can serve as your reminder to pursue God's kingdom today?

Prayer

God, today I commit to pursue Your goal, Your standard, Your kingdom. Refocus my vision and strengthen my determination. Amen.

3

A Kingdom Man

*The difference between a successful person
and others is not a lack of strength, not a lack
of knowledge, but rather a lack of will.*
—Vince Lombardi,
What It Takes to Be Number One

American life changed permanently on September 11, 2001. Terrorists hijacked jetliners and turned them into missiles, destroying New York City's Twin Towers, damaging the Pentagon, and killing thousands. The War on Terror began. In the aftermath, Arizona Cardinals safety Pat Tillman gave up a $3.6 million contract and enlisted in the Army to serve his country. He couldn't enjoy the spoils of freedom while others did the dirty work to preserve it. His sense of honor and ethics compelled him. Unfortunately Tillman's decision cost him his life. He was killed by friendly fire in Afghanistan.[1]

Men, God's kingdom will cost you your life. Jesus said, "Whoever wishes to save his life will lose it; but whoever loses his life for My sake will find it" (Matthew

16:25). A kingdom man understands that God never said a godly life would be easy; He just said it would be worth it. A kingdom man zeros in on one purpose only—advancing the kingdom for the betterment of those within it, which glorifies the King. He pursues this at whatever personal cost.

Anyone who has fought in war or battled on an athletic field knows that victory does not come just because you want it. Victory is earned only through sweat, guts, and blood, and sheer determination. It comes to those who know that purpose is far greater than pain.

APPLICATION

1. How would you describe your purpose?

2. What action can you take today to better the lives of those around you?

3. What steps can you take today to persevere in the battle?

PRAYER

God, forgive me when my body and spirit grow weak. Fill me with perseverance, no matter how great the pain. Amen.

A Kingdom Man Follows His Rule Book

*You've got to be right or wrong. I love the
satisfaction when you are right—and the
agony when you are wrong.*
—NFL referee Ed Hochuli, interview with
USA Today, October 9, 2007

Quarterback Russell Wilson released a high, arcing Hail Mary pass toward the end zone. Two Seattle Seahawks and four Green Bay Packers leaped to catch it. The crowd landed, the ball somewhere among them. One official signaled touchdown Seahawks. One official signaled interception Packers. The score stood. The Seahawks won. And the third team was the source of great controversy.[1]

The third team? The team of officials, in this case replacements being used during a labor lockout of the real refs. Their commitment and allegiance belong to a different kingdom: the NFL office. Their authority comes from a book that holds the guidelines, rules, and regulations by which they are to manage the events on the field. If an official's viewpoint leaves the book, he demotes himself to the status of a fan; he becomes illegitimate in terms of authority.

Men, you have received instructions from the League office in heaven. You have been given the Book under the authority of the Lord Jesus Christ. To rule well, to bring order to the chaos in this war called life, you must align your heart and mind with God's sovereign instruction and guidelines. You must sharpen your ear to the call of your Commissioner. You must hide His Book in your heart to rule well according to His purposes.

APPLICATION

1. What are you doing to know your rule Book?

2. How can you restore order to your domain rather than add chaos?

3. How will you align your heart with God's Word today?

PRAYER

Great Commissioner, align my head and heart with Your Word today. Shape me to Your standards and enable me to bring order as Your official. Amen.

5

A Kingdom Man Is Prepared

For 42 years, I've been making small regular deposits
in this bank of experience: education and training.
And on January 15, the balance was sufficient
so that I could make a very large withdrawal.

—US Airways Captain Chesley "Sully" Sullenberger,
in an interview with *CBS Evening News,* June 12, 2009

In January 2009, birds flew into the engines of US Airways Flight 1549 immediately after the plane's takeoff from New York's LaGuardia Airport. Both engines simultaneously shut down. The only option was to ditch the plane in the Hudson River. Doing so without accruing fatalities was unlikely—even for a veteran pilot, flight instructor, and accident investigator like Captain Chesley B. Sullenberger III.

Yet Sullenberger took charge of the realm for which he was responsible. While passengers cried out for someone to bring order to the chaos, Sullenberger kept the plane just high enough to clear the George Washington Bridge and performed a perfect textbook ditching. All souls survived in the "Miracle on the Hudson."

Captain Sullenberger had never guided an 80-ton piece of metal onto the water's surface. But he had learned aircraft maneuvering inside and out. His previous 19,000 hours of flight time had prepared him with the skills and mind-set to rule the realm of his plane well, rather than his plane ruling him.[1]

Men, the mastery of your kingdom under God's authority demands wholehearted preparation. Some moments may appear uneventful, but each is an opportunity to administer order, authority, and provision to your domain. Each day provides a choice to align your life under God's authority, to exercise and sharpen your leadership, to prepare. When chaos enters your kingdom, you will be ready.

APPLICATION

1. When has chaos taken you by surprise? How will you be ready for it next time?

2. Who is depending on you to come through when it counts?

3. How can you prepare today?

PRAYER

God of miracles, draw my heart to discipline. Give me Your vision of purpose daily. Prepare me. Amen.

6

A Kingdom Man Makes the Right Choice

Love cares more for others than
for self. . . . [Love] keeps going to the end.
—1 Corinthians 13:3–7, *The Message*

Some years ago, I heard a story about an eagle. It flew over a river one winter and noticed a large chunk of ice floating in the water. The eagle landed on the ice to relax for a minute. He had eagle eyes so he could see a waterfall up ahead. He could hear the roar of the cascading torrent downstream. But he knew he had plenty of time to fly away. So he stayed. But as the eagle stood on the ice, his talons froze to it. As he spread his wings to fly away, he went nowhere. He was stuck. He had waited too long, and he plunged over the falls on his chunk of ice.[1]

As a man, you are a leader by position and function. You are ultimately responsible for those within your domain. You can lead those under your care to safety or drive them to harm. But to sit and wait passively is a choice for destruction. Joshua chose well and ruled well, and as he neared the end of his life, he reminded his people of their choice: "Choose for yourselves today whom you will serve," he said. "But as for me and my house, we will serve the LORD" (Joshua 24:15). You must make the same choice every day. Ruling well is a lifelong skill forged through faithfulness and dedication. A kingdom man chooses daily to give his all to rule well.

APPLICATION

1. Who is your house serving?

2. Have you failed by failing to choose?

3. What step will you take today toward consistent leadership?

PRAYER

Lord, reveal the steps to turn my best intentions into consistent actions. Amen.

7

A Kingdom Man Brings Freedom

Yielding to Jesus will break every form
of slavery in any human life.
—Oswald Chambers

Adolescent male elephants have been running wild, attacking one another, other animals, and humans. Elephant aggression has become a big problem in many parts of the world in recent decades. As scientists have tried to figure out why, they've determined that elephant social structure has been destroyed, mostly due to poaching. Elder elephants are missing, especially adult male bulls, who are favorite targets of poachers. When South African park rangers flew in some adult male elephants, they flapped their ears, raised their trunks, and bellowed for days—and they restored order. The young males got in line and stopped their destruction.[1]

The same is true of humans. When men are absent or fail to lead, society erodes. It's why nearly all the inmates at the prison I visit came from homes where the father was absent, neglectful, or abusive. It's why overwhelming percentages of prisoners and high-school dropouts had absent fathers.[2] Society's problems are not just society's problems. They are the church's problems. They are our problems.

Jesus proclaimed, "He has sent Me to proclaim release to the captives" (Luke 4:18). Men, this begins in our own manhood, in our lives, in our families, and in our communities. A kingdom man finds freedom in Christ and spreads it within his realm.

APPLICATION

1. How have you been held captive? How has Christ set you free?

2. Where in your domain can you be more present?

3. To whom in your realm of influence can you bring kingdom freedom?

PRAYER

God, bring healing freedom into my life. Make me a source of healing and liberation to those in my domain. Amen.

8

A Kingdom Man Builds a Legacy

> *Father!—To God himself*
> *we cannot give a holier name.*
> —Marmaduke, in William Wordsworth's *The Borderers*

I could have been a casualty of men not fulfilling their God-given role to provide leadership and mirror God's character. My father and mother were in constant conflict. Our home was filled with chaos. Divorce seemed like the only possible outcome. But what my dad modeled for me the year I turned ten forever changed my life. That was the year my dad turned to Jesus. He immediately became fired up about God and the Bible.

My mom didn't like my dad as a sinner, and she liked him even less as a saint. She did everything she could to knock my dad's focus off of God and to make him stop loving her. But nothing worked. My dad loved her unconditionally. He was calm, consistent, and caring. Finally one night, she said, "I want what you have because it must be real."

The impact a father has on a home, a marriage, and on a church or community cannot be emphasized enough. My father's impact dramatically altered the trajectory of my life and, as a result, has impacted countless more people.

Men, you are leaving a legacy. Your choices, attitudes, and actions are shaping lives and impacting destinies. Whether you received brokenness or goodness from your own father, you are a new creation in Christ (2 Corinthians 5:17). You are able to do all things through Christ's strength (Philippians 4:13). You are a kingdom man.

APPLICATION

1. What foundation did you receive from your father?

2. What legacy are you building for those under your influence?

3. Who serves as your mentor and supports you as a man, leader, husband, or father?

PRAYER

Heavenly Father, fill me with Your unconditional love and strength. Build in and through me a legacy that declares and administers Your kingdom. Amen.

9

A Kingdom Man Rules Under God's Authority

*It is only the unworthy in [a man] that
does not bow down to the worthy.*
—Oswald Chambers, *My Utmost for His Highest*

In sports, positions define roles. You don't want your defensive tackle throwing the ball. You don't want your designated hitter pitching. And if you can help it, you don't want your center dribbling the ball up the court. But when each player is filling his position, the team works. The division of roles frees each athlete to maximize his play.

Despite the bad press the word *rule* has received from the world, a man's rule—when carried out under the overarching rule of God—is a liberating leadership for him and for those around him. The biblical concept of dominion, or rule, is neither a dictatorship nor a domination. Instead it is exercising legitimate authority under the lordship of Jesus Christ. Legitimate authority entails all that God provides for and permits a man to do—not whatever wishes or whims a man thinks he might like to do. His authority is contained by his position. Even Jesus relied on the Father for His direction, parameters, and power: "I am not here on my own authority, but he who sent me is true" (John 7:28, NIV).

Men, you are here to run God's plays. You have been put on earth to carry out God's agenda—not your own. As you submit your desires to God's authority, He will purify you, realign your heart, and equip you to rule with a leadership that elevates the game of those around you.

APPLICATION

1. Does your leadership bring glory to you or to God?

2. Which of your desires needs to be brought under Christ's authority today?

3. As God calls you today, what is your answer?

PRAYER

God, Your authority is worthy. Align my heart and desires to Yours, and enable me to rule with grace, love, and liberation. Amen.

10

A Kingdom Man Takes Responsibility

The buck stops here.
—A sign on the desk of President Harry S. Truman

If you've ever played or watched sports, you know what I mean by the "loser's limp." It's what happens when an outfielder misjudges a fly ball and misses the catch, or when a wide receiver drops an easy pass. The player falls to the ground and gets up limping. He's not really hurt. The purpose of the limp is to camouflage his failure. He wants his teammates and fans to think he missed the ball because of a cramp or pulled muscle or other injury— anything besides his own mistake. It's the athlete's excuse.[1]

Adam tried his own loser's limp way back in the garden. Despite what you learned from a Bible storybook, Eve was not alone during her conversation with the serpent. Genesis 3:6 describes "her husband with her." The whole time the serpent was talking, Adam was there. Silent. And by his silence, Adam relinquished his God-given right to leadership. The silence of Adam is still a problem among men. But Adam—and you and I—are still accountable. While Eve bore responsibility for her part, Adam was held responsible because of his leadership position.

Men, you are responsible for that which falls within your realm of influence: your family, ministry, career, resources, community, or other areas of personal influence. Stop living as a responder. Lose the loser's limp. Own up whether you make the grab or bobble the ball. And embrace your role as a kingdom leader.

APPLICATION

1. Where are you hiding in silence?

2. When have you sat back as a responder rather than moved forward with leadership.

3. How can you take responsibility for your realm today?

PRAYER

God, forgive me when I am passive and silent. Fill me with courage to embrace the role of leadership You have given me. Amen.

A Kingdom Man Has Got It

I've got it.

—Tony Evans, *Kingdom Man*

The Chicago Bulls were losing a normal, regular season game early in Michael Jordan's career. Jordan reentered the game and poured in about 25 points. The Bulls won.

As they walked off the court, assistant coach Tex Winter turned to Jordan and said, "You know, there's no *I* in team."

"There's not an *I* in team," Jordan replied. "But there's an *I* in win."[1]

Jordan and the Bulls championship dynasty still lay ahead, and it would take the contributions of entire teams to rise to their eventual dominance. But when the game was on the line, no one rose to the challenge like Jordan. He was the leader. MJ was the man.

When a problem comes up in the Evans home, I sometimes raise three fingers, which stand for three words: *I've got it.*

I'll take responsibility for it. If it's something I cannot solve, I'll provide the comfort, stability, and empathy necessary to get through it. It doesn't mean that I literally do everything. It means I see to it that everything is done.

When you demonstrate to a woman, children, or others within your sphere of influence that you are dependable, responsible, and that you take ownership to fix, solve, or simply carry the burden of that which needs to be solved, you free them to rest. You free them to relax because they know they can trust the man who has proven to them through past actions that he's got it. As a kingdom man, those around you need to know that you've got it.

APPLICATION

1. Why have you let some problems slide?

2. What problem or concern needs your attention now?

3. How can you say "I've got it" today?

PRAYER

God, fill me with Your courage and strength to free my family from worry. Help me to have it. Amen.

12

A Kingdom Man Trusts that God's Got It

Do not be afraid to take Mary as your wife.
—An angel of the Lord, Matthew 1:20

Joseph's domain suddenly turned upside down with a surreal twist. One day the small-town carpenter had a good, simple life. His career was on track. Soon he would marry and begin a family. This was the path of a good, Hebrew man. Everything was according to plan.

Until that day. Everything changed. Everything imploded into shock, shame, and betrayal. And his betrothed's only explanation was that God had made her pregnant. Unbelievable!

That's when the angel appeared with the message "Do not be afraid . . ." Essentially God intervened to say, "Don't worry, Joseph. You've got it because *I've* got it."

You can take responsibility, men, even if you don't feel as if you have the skills, wisdom, or ability to handle it. If you will align yourself under God, you can be confident He's got it. God's covering over us as His sons is a model of how we as men are to cover those under us: with protection, provision, and an environment for nurturing emotional, spiritual, and physical health.

Sometimes situations come up that make me think, *There's no way I can remedy this one. It's too deep or too chaotic, and nothing in Scripture specifically addresses these details—other than to trust God, have faith, and honor Him.* But I still hold up three fingers as if I mean it—not because I'm pretending, but because, as a man under God, I have faith that God has it.

APPLICATION

1. What problem in your life appears insurmountable?

2. How can you align yourself under God's covering?

3. What Scripture will be your reminder of God's care today?

PRAYER

God, there's no way I can handle this one—without You. Please remind me that You've got it. Amen.

13

A Kingdom Man
Longs to Be Great

Remember that this greatness was won by
men with courage, with knowledge of their
duty, and with a sense of honor in action.
—Thucydides, fifth-century Greek historian

The reasons were many why Dirk Nowitzki and the Dallas Mavericks couldn't win the 2011 NBA Championship. Nowitzki was too old (thirty-two). The Mavs had lost twenty-one of thirty-one postseason games since reaching the 2006 Finals. Many thought they'd be upset in the first round—especially after blowing a 24-point lead that allowed the Portland Trail Blazers to tie the series at two games each.

But that's when Nowitzki rose to greatness and carried his team with him. The seven-footer brought his team back to clinch several come-from-behind victories. He played with a torn tendon in his finger and a fever in Game 4 of the Finals. Even the Miami Heat, heavily favored with LeBron James and Dwyane Wade, couldn't stop Nowitzki and company.[1] The Mavericks completed their quest. Nowitzki, the Finals MVP, declared his greatness.[2]

Men long to be great. We also desire to be recognized as great. God wants you to be great as well. He has destined you to be great in His kingdom.

Greatness is maximizing your potential for the glory of God and the good of others. The apostle Paul urged those under his influence at Thessalonica to "excel still more" in how they obeyed God's commands (1 Thessalonians 4:1). He urged the Corinthians to "always [abound] in the work of the Lord" (1 Corinthians 15:58) and to seek greatness in all that they did since all that they did, according to 1 Corinthians 10:31, was to be done "to the glory of God."

Hear me when I say this—it is okay to want greatness. Be great.

APPLICATION

1. What are your dreams?

2. What has kept you from pursuing them?

3. How can you today maximize your potential for God's glory and others' good?

PRAYER

Lord, make me great for Your kingdom. Amen.

14

A Kingdom Man Finds Strength in Meekness

[A humble man] will not be thinking about humility:
he will not be thinking about himself at all.

—C. S. Lewis, *Mere Christianity*

There's a good chance you've never heard of Darwin E. Smith. As author of *Good to Great* Jim Collins says, "Despite being one of the greatest CEOs of the twentieth century, [Smith] remains largely unknown." Yet Smith quietly turned Kimberly-Clark into the number-one paper-based consumer products company in the world.

He was far from a celebrity chief executive. Instead the reserved, even shy, man preferred directing attention to the company and its people. He approached corporate leadership with humility, saying, "I never stopped trying to become qualified for the job." But Smith was not afraid to make bold decisions, such as selling Kimberly-Clark's paper mills. Such moves were ridiculed by Wall Street, yet slowly and consistently, Kimberly-Clark rose and eventually overtook competitors, including Proctor and Gamble, in market share.[1]

Darwin Smith's ambition was for the greatness of the institution, not for himself. Smith was meek.

Meekness is not weakness. Meekness simply means submitting your power to a higher Control—it means submitting yourself to God's kingdom rule. Moses understood this. Numbers 12:3 calls Moses the most humble man on earth. Because Moses was able to submit himself to divine authority, God was able to do great things in him and through him. God made Moses a great man.

Men, what you never want to do in your desire to be great is to try to steal or usurp God's glory. God is not opposed to greatness. God is opposed to pride. Big difference.

APPLICATION

1. Is your ambition for yourself or God's kingdom?

2. How would those in your sphere describe your leadership style?

3. What prideful attitudes do you need to confess?

PRAYER

God, replace my pride with humility. May my ambition be for You, not me. Amen.

A Kingdom Man Is Free to Pursue Greatness

Be not afraid of greatness: some are born
great, some achieve greatness, and some
have greatness thrust upon them.
—Shakespeare, *Twelfth Night*

Abraham recognized something special about the three strangers who appeared near his tent in the heat of the day. He moved quickly to serve them with his finest. It seems Abraham recognized God's greatness. And God used the angelic visit in Genesis 18:2–18 to affirm Abraham as a great man and a great nation.

Keep in mind this was God talking. God wanted Abraham—and others later in the Bible such as David—to be great. You may say, "But, Tony, that's Abraham. That's David. I'm just an ordinary man. God never said that to me."

Oh, but you are wrong. Jesus did in John 14:12: "He who believes in Me, the works that I do, he will do also; and greater works than these he will do."

If you have shrunk away from your innate desire for significance, you have walked into the enemy's trap. God's agenda is to advance His kingdom down the field of life; to do so, He is looking for men who will rise to the occasion in their bid for greatness.

First, you must give yourself permission to want it. You were made for greatness. It's okay to want it.

APPLICATION

1. What keeps you from believing you can be great?

2. What does the Bible say is your identity in Christ?

3. How can you shake free from the enemy's trap and step toward greatness in Christ?

PRAYER

Great God, set me free to want and pursue the greatness for which You have destined me. Amen.

16

A Kingdom Man Serves

You know that the rulers of the Gentiles lord
it over them, and their great men exercise
authority over them. It is not this way
among you, but whoever wishes to become
great among you shall be your servant.
—Jesus, Matthew 20:25–26

The brothers James and John had what might just be the most raucous nickname in the Bible: the Sons of Thunder. Can you imagine the sibling rivalry between these two? They said what they thought, no holding back. Luke 9:51–54 tells us they wanted to call down heavenly fire on a Samaritan village that rejected Jesus' message. And Matthew 20:20–28 tells us that as soon as Jesus told His disciples about His coming death and resurrection, their mother bluntly asked Jesus to give them the highest honor in His kingdom. The other disciples were ticked off, but something tells me the Sons of Thunder didn't care.

Yet Jesus never corrected the two men for what they wanted. Jesus corrected them only for how they wanted to go about accomplishing greatness. Jesus just told them not to try to get it the same way that the Gentiles did: with power plays and politics, much like our world does today.

Many men still rule by intimidation, fear tactics, and leverage. But Jesus said, "It is not this way among you." The rulers of God's kingdom are much different from the rulers of the world, as are their strategies. Jesus defined the way to get greatness as service. True greatness is outward-focused and others-driven. It is not dominance, but rather dominion that benefits those around you.

APPLICATION

1. How do you try to gain greatness?

2. Who do you know that exemplifies greatness through service?

3. What will you ask Jesus for today?

PRAYER

God, shape my vision for greatness, and use me in Your service today. Amen.

A Kingdom Man
Plays His Position

There are many parts, but one body.
—Apostle Paul, 1 Corinthians 12:20, NIV

It's easy to make jokes about punters in the NFL. After all, they're not usually the biggest, brawniest guys in the sport of gladiatorial combat. But any smart football player, coach, or fan will tell you that a punter is one of the greatest players on the team.

The Oakland Raiders grasped this truth so deeply that they used their 1973 first-round draft pick to select punter Ray Guy. And it was a pick well made. Guy is still widely considered the greatest punter ever. His high looping kicks inspired the creation of the NFL statistics category *hang time*. He was the first to hit a TV screen above the Louisiana Superdome, and one opposing coach once swiped one of Guy's footballs and had it tested for helium. In his fourteen-year career, only three of Guy's punts were blocked; none was ever returned for a touchdown.

Even better than most punters, Guy could pin opponents into the worst possible field position. He changed the momentum—and outcomes—of many a game. Guy achieved greatness on the football field.[1]

The greatest player on any team, whether a corporate, family, ministry, or sports team, is the player who makes certain that his contribution best fits within the goals and strategies of the team. You may be a quarterback, defensive end, or punter in the game of life. But known or unknown, you need to be great. Greatness for a kingdom man begins by aligning yourself with God's kingdom agenda to benefit others.

Decide today that you want greatness and that you will pursue it according to God's methods.

APPLICATION

1. What position has God given you the skills to play?

2. Are you seeking recognition or greatness?

3. What play do you need to execute today?

PRAYER

God, show me my position on Your team and sharpen my skills for greatness. Amen.

18

A Kingdom Man Stops Making Excuses

After him came Shamgar the son of Anath,
who struck down six hundred Philistines
with an oxgoad; and he also saved Israel.
—Judges 3:31

One man. One verse. Ten seconds for you to read about him. A lifetime of change if you grasp his important lessons. Shamgar.

His name alone sounds like a superhero. Pronounce it slowly: *Sh-am-ga-rr.* You can almost hear the growl at the end. There is power in that name. Shamgar himself had power.

But Shamgar was most likely an ordinary farmer trying to provide for his family at a time when the enemy Philistines terrorized the nation of Israel. Shamgar wasn't a military man or a politician. Shamgar didn't wait until things were easy to do something on behalf of his nation. He didn't put off until next week what he needed to do that day. Shamgar didn't wait until he became great to do something great. Shamgar saved the entire nation of Israel—as a farmer.

Men, life may not be what you want it to be. I understand that life has challenges. But the first lesson in becoming a kingdom man of influence and impact is to stop making excuses.

If you are a farmer and that is all you know how to do, then ask God how He wants you to use your farming to influence and impact the realm you live in now. Don't wait until you become a big shot to do big-shot things.

APPLICATION

1. What excuses have you been allowing to limit you?

2. What whisper in your heart have you been answering with "yeah, but . . ."?

3. What small step toward big-shot things can you take today?

PRAYER

God, forgive my excuses. My answer is yes. Guide my steps and strengthen my hands in Your service. Amen.

19

A Kingdom Man Advances One Step at a Time

*I remember later reading our yearbook about
the unbeaten season and thinking, . . .
What if I didn't make the 54-yarder?*
—Garo Yepremian, on his 1992 Game-6 winning field goal

Will there ever be another perfect NFL season? Each passing year makes it seem less likely that any team will match the 17-win, 0-loss championship run of the 1972 Miami Dolphins. The 2007 New England Patriots came closest, reaching the Super Bowl with 19 straight victories, but then fell to a stunning comeback by the New York Giants.

How did the Dolphins do what no other team has done in nearly one hundred years of pro football? One game, one play at a time. Even when the Dolphins eventual Hall of Fame quarterback Bob Griese left Game 5—and stayed out eight games—due to a broken leg, the Dolphins pulled together and applied their will to advance down the field, over all opponents, one step, one yard at a time toward greatness.

It's the same strategy Shamgar used to take down 600 Philistines. He used what he had—an oxgoad, a farming tool no less—to triumph one man at a time (Judges 3:31).

Men, your overall goal may feel insurmountable, but don't fall into excuses that keep you from doing anything at all. Take each challenge one step at a time, one day at a time, one project at a time. You will be amazed at where you eventually wind up.

Application

1. What's your long-term goal?

2. What are the small steps on the road to reaching it?

3. What one step will you take to advance today?

Prayer

Father, let Your Word be a light to my path today. Reveal my next step and enable me to take it. Amen.

20

A Kingdom Man Makes the Most of What He Has

Do what you can, with what you have, where you are.
—Theodore Roosevelt

Wally Amos began his career in the mailroom of the William Morris Agency, the world's largest and oldest talent agency. He eventually worked his way up to become the firm's first African-American agent. His trademark was sending homemade cookies along with his invitations to new business prospects. The recipe was his own, honed while he had attended Food Trades Vocational High School.

The cookies were so good that celebrities Marvin Gaye and Helen Reddy gave Amos a loan to launch his first Famous Amos store in 1975. In less than a decade, Famous Amos cookies were a multimillion-dollar success story.[1]

Men, never let your limitations limit what God can do with you, even if you are, for now, in the mailroom.

If you will simply make the most of where you are, God will do the rest. He is watching to see what you will do first with what He has already given you when no one else is paying that much attention.

When you look a little closer at what you have, you may discover, like Shamgar or Moses or David, that you have more than enough to accomplish God's plan for you. Yes, you may be limited in resources or even in skills, but while God doesn't always call the equipped, He always equips the called.

Never look at only what you have. Look at what it can become. Use what you have right now to step toward what God has destined you for.

APPLICATION

1. What's one thing you're good at?

2. What is one way God has worked in your life?

3. What skill, resource, or gift has God entrusted you with to use today?

PRAYER

Lord, teach me to maximize every gift, no matter how small, for Your kingdom. Amen.

21

A Kingdom Man Chooses to Be the One

*Remember . . . all I'm offering
is the truth—nothing more.*
—Morpheus, in *The Matrix*

Thomas A. Anderson sits in the sparse, shadowy room trying to orient himself to the strange events happening to him. Driven by boredom and unrest, the ordinary computer programmer had turned to hacking in search of something more exciting or meaningful.

Now a mysterious figure named Morpheus sits in front of him, calling him Neo, explaining that the Matrix is a lie. The Matrix is a program to blind him from the truth and to keep him from discovering a truth unseen. Morpheus offers a choice. Take a blue pill and remain the bored and ordinary Thomas A. Anderson. Take the red pill and enter the reality of Neo, savior of a deeper realm.

Morpheus says, "Follow me."[1]

Those words from the movie *The Matrix* are the same words offered by Jesus—to His twelve disciples

2000 years ago, to you, and to me today.

"Follow Me" (Matthew 4:19).

The choice is yours. You can take the red pill—the pill that has been offered, infused with the power and authority given to you by the blood of Jesus Christ—and you can be ushered into your call to greatness. Or you can take the other pill, only to live out the remainder of your ordinary existence.

You are the one.

You are the one to make a difference in your destiny, your family, church, work, community, our nation, and around the world.

The choice is yours. Be the one.

APPLICATION

1. How have you answered Jesus' call to "Follow Me"?

2. What is the choice facing you today that can change your destiny?

3. Which pill will you take?

PRAYER

God, I choose You. I choose Your kingdom. Lead me forward. I am Your one. Amen.

A Kingdom Man Is Heroic

*His delight is in the law of the LORD, and in His
law he meditates day and night. He will be like
a tree firmly planted by streams of water, which
yields its fruit in its season and its leaf does not
wither; and in whatever he does, he prospers.*

—Psalm 1:2–3

As the clock ticked to all zeroes, the 1958 NFL Championship Game between the Baltimore Colts and the New York Giants was knotted 17–17.[1] Until then, regular season NFL games that ended in a tie remained just that. But this was a Championship Game, in a nationally televised sport trying to gain fans in a nation obsessed with baseball.

My eight-year-old eyes stared at the screen, waiting with millions across the nation. In an unprecedented move, the officials announced that the game would go into overtime. For the first time in NFL history, a game went to sudden death.[2] And in the thriller since dubbed "The Greatest Game Ever Played,"[3] the Colts triumphed.

Because I grew up in Baltimore, these Colts were my team. Colts halfback Lenny Moore was my childhood sports hero, and he had been one of the first black men to claim the NFL Rookie of the Year a few seasons before.[4] The game in my neighborhood was football as my friends and I pretended to be Moore, or Johnny Unitas, or Raymond Berry.

Ask any man, and he'll rattle off a name, or two, or ten of "heroes" he looked up to as a kid. The accomplishments of men inspire boys to become like them. Men, whether you are a father or not, there are eyes upon you, watching, learning, seeking inspiration and example. The influence of a kingdom man shows up in the lives under his influence and care.

APPLICATION

1. Who were your childhood heroes?

2. Who is watching you?

3. What example can you live today?

PRAYER

Father, make me a worthy role model, pointing toward Your kingdom. Amen.

23

A Kingdom Man Rejects False Manhood

Therefore if anyone is in Christ, he is a new creature; the old things passed away; behold, new things have come.
—2 Corinthians 5:17

Gordon Gekko paced to the front of the crowded stockholders meeting, his voice rising with fervor. "Greed, for lack of a better word, is good. Greed is right. Greed works," Gekko said. In the movie *Wall Street*, Gekko claimed to be a liberator of companies, not a destroyer of them. But the ruthless corporate raider was driven by his own greed, and his illegal insider trading tactics landed him in prison.[1]

Gekko has remained a pop-culture symbol of unrestrained desire, and he represents well the *Corporate Man:* a male who defines manhood by the time he invests in his career and/or by the amount of money he can accrue. But there are many false definitions of manhood within our culture, including the following:

Passive Man: A male is who is unable or unwilling to take the leadership role that God has assigned him.

Domineering Man: Thinks manhood is measured by his ability to emotionally and/or physically force compliance to his demands.

Sexual Man: Measures his manhood by the number of women he can conquer.

Irresponsible Man: Refuses to provide properly for the well-being of those under his care.

Hedonistic Man: Lives for self-gratifying pleasure at the expense of those around him.

Only when a man functions as a biblical kingdom man will he experience the fullness of his destiny. Men, you must set aside the false man and embrace the true.

APPLICATION

1. What false definition of manhood have you accepted?

2. What kingdom man character do you want to play in life?

3. How can you walk as a "new creature" today?

PRAYER

God, help me to turn my back on the old things and walk forward as the new man You have made me. Amen.

24

A Kingdom Man Realigns

This book of the law shall not depart from your
mouth, but you shall meditate on it day and night,
so that you may be careful to do according to all
that is written in it; for then you will make your
way prosperous, and then you will have success.

—Joshua 1:8

I took my car in for its routine oil change and got a call from the dealership telling me they had discovered another issue. My tires were not wearing evenly. The problem, though, wasn't with my tires. The problem was with my vehicle's alignment. The mechanic told me, "If I don't fix the alignment, you will end up with the same problem on your new tires." Replacing my worn-out tires would not have solved my problem.

When we look around our world today, we can see a lot of wear and tear—on women, children, churches, communities, and our nation. But, men, we don't have a wife, family, kids, community, or job problem. We have a man problem. As harsh as this may sound, it boils down to you. And it boils down to me. Men, we must align ourselves with the purposes of God's kingdom.

We must fine-tune our heads and our hearts daily, recentering them on the truth of God's Word, checking them from being pulled off course. When Joshua was entrusted with the leadership of the Israelites after Moses' death, he was told to hold fast to God's law, to not turn away to the left or right. We share the same call and the same promise: success in God's kingdom as we align ourselves to God's true direction.

APPLICATION

1. In which direction is your heart pulling you off course?

2. When is the last time you recalibrated your heart?

3. What do you need to do to realign yourself today to God's kingdom?

PRAYER

Lord, You are truth. Make my paths straight and my heart true. Amen.

25

A Kingdom Man
Acts His Age

*In short, in life, as in a football game, the
principle to follow is: Hit the line hard; don't
foul and don't shirk, but hit the line hard!*
—Theodore Roosevelt, "The American Boy"

Theodore Roosevelt had already served as president of
the United States from 1901 to 1909. But he was back
campaigning as the Progressive Party candidate for the
1912 election when he was shot in the chest in an as-
sassination attempt. Roosevelt finished his speech before
seeing a doctor ninety minutes later.

It was classic Roosevelt, America's most cowboy president. Roosevelt's robust personality and strong leadership
restored the strength of the American presidency and led
the nation to world prominence. The chief executive was
equally known as a warrior, environmental activist, big
game hunter, and prolific writer.

But as a boy, Roosevelt had been sickly and forced
to stay indoors due to severe asthma. Doctors also told

him he had a weak heart and advised him to get a desk job that wouldn't strain him. "Teedie" devoted himself to studying nature, then as a teen turned to rigorous exercise to strengthen himself. Clearly, he never shied away from "strain."[1]

Men, Teddy Roosevelt understood the words of the apostle Paul: "When I was a child, I used to speak like a child, think like a child, reason like a child; when I became a man, I did away with childish things" (1 Corinthians 13:11). We must do the same, moving beyond the *male-hood* of our birth and the *boyhood* of our immaturity and dependence. We must act our age by embracing the responsibility of *manhood*—kingdom manhood.

APPLICATION

1. What 'hood are you living in?

2. What immature or irresponsible decision—or lack of decision—do you need to make right with God and others?

3. How can you act your age today?

PRAYER

God, give me the strength and discipline to live with responsibility and honor. Amen.

26

A Kingdom Man Owns Up Beyond the Bedroom

Sex is the most wonderful thing on this earth
. . . as long as God is in it. When the Devil gets
in it, it's the most terrible thing on this earth.
—Billy Graham, *Just As I Am*

Unfortunately, celebrities who have fathered multiple illegitimate children with multiple women have become so common it's cliché. A quick Internet search turns up lists of professional athletes and entertainers who have had children with numerous women. But this problem isn't limited to famous men.

Forty percent of all of the children born in America are being brought into fatherless homes—72 percent of black children.[1] Men, women are not getting themselves pregnant. This is a man problem. It's a national problem. And the root is causing many marital problems. Too many men are trying to live in male-hood and boyhood, rather than walking in manhood. And in this harmful combination of irresponsibility and dependence, too many men are demanding sexual fulfillment based on sexual identity alone.

The result is a nation of neglected and broken children—along with conflicting and confusing relational standards that lead many wives to feel used. What woman wants to be intimate with someone whom she has to clean up after, wake up for church or work, and babysit? If he can be a man in bed, then why can't he be a man in the living room, at the office, with the finances, as a father, or in the marital relationship? It's a fair question—and one kingdom men must answer with consistency and responsibility.

APPLICATION

1. Have you failed to own your life responsibilities?

2. How can you love and serve your wife today? If you're not married, how can you prepare yourself to be a kingdom man a kingdom woman would desire?

3. How can you lead your wife (or lead your future wife) to intimacy by covering her with the care of a kingdom man?

PRAYER

Father, align my sexual desires with my identity as Your kingdom man, virile and responsible. Amen.

27

A Kingdom Man Aligns His Attitude

Win or lose, this is my prayer—I want
to make sure that I make God's name great.
—Tony Dungy, quoted in *Kingdom Man*

It's common for Super Bowl champions to be invited to the White House to meet and receive congratulations from the president of the United States, but the event brought tears to Tony Dungy's eyes in April 2007. Tony's father had taught just miles from the White House in unequal, racially segregated schools. Now Tony was receiving the full presidential fanfare as the first African-American coach to win a Super Bowl.

Tony's path to the Super Bowl was a long, hard road filled with obstacles and challenges, but Tony's father taught him never to complain. Tony's dad worked as a teacher in a racially segregated and separate-but-not-equal school system with unequal tools and facilities, but he held true to his calling to train students on as equal a level as he could. Tony's father modeled the responsibility of manhood despite opposition. He took responsibility for what he could control while waiting on God to change the situations he could not. Tony's father lived aligned under God and responsible over those within his care. His son Tony has risen to great heights, and he has likewise championed God's kingdom in his home, on the football field, and in the culture at large.

Men, you may never win a Super Bowl, but you can shape and influence future champions. You can pass on a legacy of truly great kingdom men and women. Start by carrying out your divine reason for being by aligning yourself with God and His kingdom.

APPLICATION

1. What are you complaining about?

2. What part of your problems or struggles can you control?

3. How can you align your attitude to God's kingdom today?

PRAYER

Father, forgive my complaints. Shape my attitude and align me to Your will. Amen.

28

A Kingdom Man Puts Women and Children First

Greater love has no one than this,
that one lay down his life for his friends.
—John 15:13

On February 26, 1852, the British Royal Navy ship *HMS Birkenhead* carrying 643 people struck a sunken rock off the coast of South Africa. The iron-hulled, paddle steamer carried mostly military personnel, but a number of wives and children had come along on this peacetime journey.

It was quickly apparent that the *Birkenhead* would sink. Precedent on military vessels had been that in times of emergencies during a war, it was every man for himself. But Captain Robert Salmond, along with his right-hand man, Lieutenant-Colonel Alexander Seton, ordered their men to stand fast while they filled the three working lifeboats with the women and children first. Many good men lost their lives that day so that every woman and child on board could keep theirs. And "women and children first" instantly became the protocol for all future maritime emergencies around the world.[1]

Men, it is our responsibility to see to it that those under our care have every opportunity possible for protection, provision, and safety. As we align our lives with Christ, we must put first the needs of those within our realm of influence. Are we willing to lay down our lives as Christ has done for us—not only in times of emergency but on a daily basis, regardless of the cost? Christ our leader has given us a charge. It is time to stand fast.

APPLICATION

1. What would you have done on board the *HMS Birkenhead?*

2. How does your life reflect an others-first mentality?

3. How can you place first the needs of those under your care today?

PRAYER

Father, forgive my selfishness. Fill me with love and courage to serve those You have placed under my care. Amen.

29

A Kingdom Man Is a Hero

You [Lois Lane] wrote that the world
doesn't need a savior, yet everyday I
hear people crying out for one.
—Superman, in *Superman Returns*

Batman had the ultimate array of crime-fighting tools and gadgets—plus a loyal sidekick. Spider-Man had his webs and acrobatic abilities. Captain America was the peak of human performance with a patriotic mission. But none of them was mightier than Superman.

Superman had it all: flight, strength, speed, x-ray vision, and a moral compass unwavering from justice. As a schoolboy, I wanted to *be* Superman. I wanted a life that brought good to others, fought the bad guys, rescued the weak, and captured Lois's heart with every adventure.

Superman was not from this earth. And, kingdom man, neither are you. Scripture states clearly that you have been seated with Christ in the heavenly realm (Ephesians 2:6). Because of this, you operate with a kingdom set of rules backed by kingdom authority that has the power, when used correctly, to transform your ordinary life into an extraordinary one. That means more than being a great football player, a great businessman, a successful community leader, or a wealthy individual. Being a kingdom man involves being the hero who aligns himself under the headship and authority of Jesus Christ so he can fully access the power and authority of Jesus Christ to positively influence and impact everything and everyone within his realm.

Men, model yourself after the greatest Kingdom Man of all who over two thousand years ago rescued a world in distress.

APPLICATION

1. What superpower do you wish you had?

2. What wrong do you need to right?

3. How can you follow Christ and bring aid or justice to those in your realm today?

PRAYER

Father, I am a broken, imperfect man without You. Fill me with Your power and the wisdom to use it. Amen.

30

A Kingdom Man Readies Himself for Judgment

Each one of us will give an account of himself to God.
—Romans 14:12

Two relatively unknown athletes rocketed to superstardom in the buildup to the 1992 Olympics in Barcelona, Spain. Dan O'Brien was the reigning US and world decathlon champion, and Dave Johnson was a three-time US champion. But decathlon is an obscure sport. Not many people had heard of them.

That all changed in thirty seconds when Reebok launched its $25 million advertising campaign during the Super Bowl. The commercials asked, "Who is the world's greatest athlete? Dan or Dave? To be settled in Barcelona." Suddenly the two athletes became full-fledged celebrities recognized by fans wearing red Dan shirts or blue Dave ones.

The problem was that neither had yet qualified for the Olympics, and at the US trials, the unthinkable happened. Dan failed to qualify in the pole-vault event. He didn't make the team; he didn't go to the Olympics. A foregone conclusion went bust.

Men, you will be tested. No one gets off without a test. We all will face judgment. Both 2 Corinthians 5:10 and Romans 14:10–12 mention standing before the judgment seat, or *bema* as the apostle Paul called it. What is revealed at the bema is whether you were a kingdom man on earth, properly aligned under Jesus Christ, or whether you were an earthly man. How well you lived in light of advancing God's cause in history will determine the rights and privileges granted to you during the one-thousand-year kingdom reign of Christ. Live as a champion now and prove yourself worthy of greater feats in God's future service.

APPLICATION

1. How is your spiritual fitness?

2. How would you fare standing before Christ today?

3. What step toward kingdom discipline and training can you take today?

PRAYER

Heavenly Father, help me rise to the challenges and be found worthy in Your service. Amen.

31

A Kingdom Man
Imitates Christ

Imitation is the sincerest of flattery.
—Charles Caleb Colton, *Lacon, Vol. I*

His story is unbelievable. That's why it made such a compelling movie and Broadway musical. But the real life experiences behind *Catch Me If You Can* are true. After Frank Abagnale ran away from home at age sixteen, he began scamming his way into big money. He eventually passed himself off as an airline pilot, doctor, lawyer, and college professor, and he forged and cashed $2.5 million dollars in bad checks along the way. Eventually he got caught and sent to prison. Today Abagnale advises the FBI on, you guessed it, forgery, embezzlement, and secure documents.

Frank Abagnale was a master imitator. You should be too. Paul wrote in 1 Corinthians 11, "Be imitators of me, just as I also am of Christ. . . . I want you to understand that Christ is the head of every man, and the man is the head of a woman, and God is the head of Christ" (1, 3).

You can't get much more basic than that. Christ is the head of every man.

The man is the head of a woman.

And God is the head of Christ.

This is foundational to kingdom living and ruling. Paul said that we must start with the basics of alignment and headship. And that begins by imitating Christ. Men, how much does your life look like Jesus? How focused are you on imitating your King? It all starts here.

APPLICATION

1. Who is your life imitating?

2. What do you find difficult and easy to imitate in Christ?

3. How can you imitate Jesus today?

PRAYER

Lord, mold my life to be like Yours. Let others see You in me. Amen.

32

A Kingdom Man
Accepts His Role

I have come down from heaven, not to do My own will, but the will of Him who sent Me.
—Jesus (John 6:38)

He knew exactly what was coming. He understood the plan. More than we can imagine, Jesus grasped the depths of suffering and agony He would have to endure to pay humanity's debt to restore us to the Father. And He cried out for some other way—any other way—as blood mixed with sweat seeping through his fully human pores in the Garden of Gethsemane. We can identify with Jesus' physical suffering. We can shudder at our worst bodily pain multiplied to deadly levels: the beatings, the whippings, the piercings, the brutality of the cross. But we cannot fathom the intensity of the spiritual suffering of bearing every single act of grotesque sin throughout history.

If ever there was an illustration of the crucial nature and accomplishment of biblical headship, Calvary was it. Jesus was able to function in alignment at Calvary, in the heat of the battle, because He held an accurate understanding and practice of it prior to Calvary. Jesus and the Father are one (John 10:30), but when it came to functioning on Earth, Jesus came under God to carry out the divine plan.

Headship isn't about essence or being; it is about function. Headship doesn't determine or reflect a lack of equality. It doesn't deny oneness. Rather, it defines roles. Men, the same is true in our homes and marriages.

APPLICATION

1. What functions are you and your wife carrying out in your home? If you're not married, what functions would you take on if you were?

2. How can you be (or prepare to be) a better head in your home?

3. How do you need to surrender to Christ as your head?

PRAYER

Father, I surrender to Your authority. Help me live out my role with love and grace. Amen.

33

A Kingdom Man Understands His Boundary

Authority without wisdom is like a heavy axe
without an edge, fitter to bruise than polish.
—Anne Bradstreet, "Meditations Divine and Moral"

Rick Carlisle is one of the best coaches in the NBA. In his ten-year NBA coaching career, Carlisle's teams have missed the postseason only once. His work guiding the Dallas Mavericks through the 2011 postseason is arguably his finest. Carlisle and his staff drew up game plans that ousted the two-time defending champion Lakers and ultimately shut down the insanely talented Miami Heat in the finals.[1] Carlisle knows how to maximize his players' talents.

But imagine what would have happened if Carlisle would have begun dictating plays to the Lakers or Heat. Kobe Bryant's and LeBron James's reactions would've been comical if Carlisle had begun ordering them around the court. Carlisle is a master of his domain, but his authority is over the Mavs only.

Men, the same is true of headship. The often controversial 1 Corinthians 11:3 states that the man is the head of *a* woman, not the head of *all* women. This is not a blanket ticket for male domination; rather this is a hierarchical structure for the home and church.[2]

It also means a man's authority is not absolute. It is valid only as long as it is consistent with the Word of God. You can't tell your wife to rob a bank, then hold her guilty for not submitting if she doesn't do it. Your authority must be placed directly under the authority of Jesus Christ.

APPLICATION

1. What do you think is the importance of "as to the Lord" in Ephesians 5:22?

2. Have you overreached the boundaries of your headship? How? Or what would be an area in which you could be tempted to overreach?

3. What is the game plan for your family (or family to-be)?

PRAYER

God, forgive me if I have misused my role. Realign my heart. Amen.

34

A Kingdom Man Brings Out the Sun

Kindness affects more than severity.
—Aesop, "The Wind and the Sun"

The sun and the wind were arguing about who was stronger. So they decided to settle the feud with a contest. Whoever could get a traveler below to remove his coat would win. The wind blew hard and fierce, but the traveler only pulled his coat tighter, hunkering within it against the cold blasts. When the sun's turn came, it radiated its full warmth and heat. The traveler loosened his coat around his neck. He unbuttoned it. And finally feeling warmed and uplifted, he removed the layer altogether.

It's an old fable, one you've undoubtedly heard, but one that applies well to headship. Men, women were designed to respond. But what you need to know about a woman is that just as much as she can receive and respond positively, she can also receive and respond negatively. If the wrong things are said or done to her, she may react in a way that reflects what is being done to her. She is a mirror reflecting to you the impact and influence that you, or other males, have had on her.

If you want a summer wife, men, then don't bring home winter weather. But if you have a winter wife, men, then it is time to bring out the sun.

APPLICATION

1. What negative responses have you been receiving from your wife?

2. How can you change your actions to reflect more positive responses? If you're single, how can you prepare to be a positive person?

3. How can you bring out the sun today?

PRAYER

Father, forgive any bitterness I have developed or influenced. Help me to convey Your love and grace. Amen.

35

A Kingdom Man
Is Consistent

How poor are they that have not patience!
What wound did ever heal but by degrees?
—Iago, in Shakespeare's *Othello*

The Chinese bamboo plant can make the average seed look like it overdosed on Miracle-Gro. Farmers must water, fertilize, and tend the seeds of this variety of bamboo throughout the year—but nothing breaks the surface of the soil for a year.

However, once this bamboo gets going, it grows at a dramatic pace, sometimes adding four feet in a single day.[1] Within weeks, it can tower seventy feet tall, anchored by the elaborate root system it developed while it appeared to do nothing.

Men, maximizing the power of your influence in the home can take time too—especially if biblical manhood has been absent. A woman needs to be sure biblical manhood is real when it does show up. She is not going to expose herself in a vulnerable manner just because you say you heard a sermon, read a book, went to a conference, or had a great morning devotion. Patience and consistency are key. Give time for the roots of security to grow deep.

When she hears you say, "I've got it"; when you lead with compassion, consistency, and wisdom; when you involve her in every significant decision; and when you value her input and desires, you will discover that your relationship will go to a level you never dreamed possible. Stay patient. Be consistent. Don't give up. Cover her in such a way that she is free to respond well.

APPLICATION

1. How long have you lived outside of your role as a kingdom man?

2. What patterns may take some time to change? Or, if you're single, what positive patterns can you develop?

3. What Scripture can be your reminder to love and lead with patience and consistency?

PRAYER

God, Your love is unending. Help me to consistently live and lead with unconditional love. Amen.

36

A Kingdom Man Rejects a Double Standard

Hypocrisy is the most difficult and nerve-
racking vice that any man can pursue; . . . It
cannot, like adultery or gluttony, be practiced
at spare moments; it is a whole-time job.
—W. Somerset Maugham, *Cakes and Ale*

A rich man and a poor man were neighbors. The rich man had made his fortune in livestock, and his herds were countless. The only good fortune the poor man knew came from a Chinese cookie. He had one lamb that his family had raised like a pet. One day the rich man thought lamb would make the perfect meal for a visitor, but he didn't want to waste one of his own. He had the poor man's pet slaughtered and roasted.

This was roughly the story the prophet Nathan told King David, and David was outraged at the injustice. He was ready to have the rich man killed—after he forced him to pay the poor man four times the value of the lamb. Of course, then Nathan delivered the punch line: "You are the man!" he told David, confronting him about his adultery with Bathsheba and the murder of her husband (2 Samuel 12:7).

David had been living a double standard. He was ready to bring the full extent of the law down on the fictional rich man while he had literally gotten away with murder. Men, to demand a woman submit to your headship while you are not willing to submit to the headship of Christ is a double standard. A man covers a woman because Christ covers a man. You cannot expect everyone to answer to you without your having to answer to anyone else.

APPLICATION

1. How have you been living a double standard?

2. What demands have you made that you haven't been willing to fulfill?

3. How can you answer to God's headship today?

PRAYER

God, forgive me for demanding a standard that I have failed to follow. Guide me in following Your headship. Amen.

37

A Kingdom Man
Belongs to a Church

No man is an island, entire of itself; every man
is a piece of the continent, a part of the main.
—John Donne, *Devotions upon Emergent Occasions*

King Arthur's court was filled with heroes. Lancelot, Galahad, Percival, and the other Knights of the Round Table roamed far and wide on noble, dangerous quests to protect the weak and to defend honor, dignity, and all that was good and just. When the kingdom operated as it should, the knights served the greater good in the service of their king. They gathered in Arthur's court at the round table designed to ensure unity, equality, and accountability. Each knight was a bold, mighty warrior. Yet he swore allegiance to his king and served shoulder to shoulder with his brothers in arms and honor.

The church is the Round Table of a kingdom man. The church is the body and fullness of Christ, and a man who is not under the leadership and guidance of the local church is not living under the headship of Christ. Within a fully operational church, the guidance and assistance that men need to maximize their biblical manhood come in many forms, including teaching, personal ministry, fellowship, and encouragement. For some men, personal discipleship needs may be so high that they need additional and deeper accountability. No kingdom man can go it alone. When men begin to function in their homes, accountable to the guidance and direction of a leader in the church, things change.

APPLICATION

1. What church leaders know you by name?

2. In what ways are you involved at church?

3. To what opportunity will you answer yes to connect with and draw strength from a local church today?

PRAYER

Father, humble me and guide me into greater accountability and support. Amen.

38

A Kingdom Man
Is a Pastor

*I will give you shepherds after My
own heart, who will feed you on
knowledge and understanding.*
—Jeremiah 3:15

Imagine the room filled with friends, families, neighbors, and strangers, gathered in their Sunday finest, seated shoulder to shoulder, waiting. For some it's been a struggle to get there. They've woken early and wrestled reluctant children into clean clothes and minivans, their patience and godly attitudes tested by the realities of life. But they are here. They have answered a longing to be filled—to touch God and be touched by Him. They wait, but there is no pastor. No leader rises to guide them.

How many people would return to this church if the pastor showed up only every three or four months?

Men, you are your wife's pastor. The church is to be where you gather the truths of God's Word to take home to your family and teach them in more detail. It is your job to hunt down answers for your wife or children.

A major component of being a pastor comes in thinking about what people under your care need to grow spiritually. As your wife's pastor, you need to intentionally consider what she needs to mature in her walk with Christ—then take steps to provide those things. The role of pastor involves shepherding, consistent discipleship, mediation, counseling (lending an empathetic and wise ear), and oversight. Men, you can create an environment where your wife looks to you for spiritual leadership and covering.

APPLICATION

1. What roles of a pastor are you providing for your family? Or, how can you prepare to become a pastor to your future family?

2. What spiritual responsibilities can you improve?

3. How will you shepherd (or prepare to shepherd) your family today?

PRAYER

God, give me the heart and hands to pastor my family (or my future family) in Your ways. Amen.

39

A Kingdom Man Roars

I feel I am going to roar.
You had better put your fingers in your ears.

—Aslan, in C. S. Lewis's *The Lion,*
the Witch and the Wardrobe

Aslan was alive. "When he opened his mouth to roar his face became so terrible that they did not dare to look at it. And they saw all the trees in front of him bend before the blast of his roaring as grass bends in a meadow before the wind."[1] As the Christ-figure in C. S. Lewis's classic tale, Aslan was back from the dead. And after a playfully loving reunion with Lucy and Susan, the mighty lion now declared his dominion over all the land. The White Witch's days were numbered.

Nothing compares to the majesty of a lion. A lion's roar carries enough force to extend five miles—that's the length of 88 football fields or 283 professional basketball courts! It would take a Ferrari racing at top speeds nearly two minutes to cross it! A lion roars to warn intruders, startle prey, reunite scattered pride members, and attract a female. But most of all, a lion roars to declare dominion.

Men, when was the last time you roared? When was the last time the reassuring strength of your roar was heard and felt by all those within your sphere of influence and under your care? When was the last time the force of your roar firmly warded off all those seeking to devour that which is within your domain? To protect, provide, lead, partner well, and express your authority within your domain, you must roar.

APPLICATION

1. When did you stop roaring?

2. What's the difference between a roar of anger and a roar of dominion?

3. What area of life needs your roar today?

PRAYER

God, give air to my lungs. Give me voice to sound Your roar. Amen.

40

A Kingdom Man Finds Power in the Word

Everyone who hears these words of Mine and does not act on them, will be like a foolish man who built his house on the sand.

—Jesus (Matthew 7:26)

I noticed recently that the lost and found area at my church seemed to be growing. Either people don't know they have lost something, or they don't care about whatever it is that has been lost. Most of the things are Bibles. These Bibles have sat there for an inordinate amount of time unclaimed, and therefore, unused.

Many men need to visit God's "lost and found" to reclaim the power of the Word of God in their lives so they can exercise it. Far too many men have misplaced their ability to maximize truths found in God's Word. They have misplaced what is absolutely essential to carry out their purpose, the fulfillment of their destiny, and the justification of their significance. As a result, they have difficulty locating, understanding, and fulfilling their right to rule.

Men, the Word of God is "living and active and sharper than any two-edged sword" (Hebrews 4:12). It is your weapon and your guide. Lose it and you wander lost. Lose connection with its power and you inadvertently become ruled by circumstance, people around you, or problems. Rather than being the head, you become the tail, wagged by life's storms or distractions. Rediscover the power of God's Word and rediscover your spiritual authority.

APPLICATION

1. When did you last experience the power of God's Word?

2. What scripture has moved or challenged you lately?

3. What book in the Bible will you begin reading today?

PRAYER

God, teach me—remind me—how to maximize the truths of Your Word. Open its power to me today. Amen.

41

A Kingdom Man
Tends His Garden

Where you tend a rose, my lad,
a thistle cannot grow.
—Frances Hodgson Burnett, *The Secret Garden*

The old, weathered gardener shouted at Mary and Colin as he climbed the ladder over the wall into *The Secret Garden* of classic literature. The children's haven had been discovered by its former caretaker. But as the old man raged, a new strength grew inside young Colin, an authority he had never realized. The boy had been confined to a wheelchair, declared crippled, and neglected by his father who was still blinded by grief after his wife's death. Now the boy cast off the blankets and robes swaddling him and the lies that bound him. He stood, straight and strong. "I'm your master," he said, "when my father is away. And you are to obey me. This is my garden."[1] Young Colin declared his dominion. He stepped into his identity. He would tend this plot of earth and find life and healing in his role there.

Men, the realm of your responsibility, your dominion, is your garden. When God spoke creation into being with His Word, He placed Adam in a garden to tend and guard it. He created man and woman in His image and stamped them with His authority to rule, with men called to leadership. This is your identity. This is your authority, given to you by your Creator. Because of whose you are, you can tend your garden with confidence and strength.

APPLICATION

1. How have you believed a crippling lie?

2. What will it take to shake off your wounds and excuses?

3. How will you tend your garden with authority today?

PRAYER

Creator, reveal Your stamp of authority in me and empower me to garden with purpose. Amen.

42

A Kingdom Man Is a Delegate

When expectations are not met,
I understand changes must be made.

—Gene Chizik, in a letter to the
"Auburn Family," November 25, 2012

The Auburn Tigers had their backs against the wall late in the fourth quarter—again. Led by Heisman Trophy-winning quarterback Cam Newton, the Tigers had pulled out dramatic comeback victories all season long. Now if they were going to claim Auburn's first national championship in fifty-three years, they would have to do it again. The Oregon Ducks had overcome a deficit to tie the game with 2:33 remaining in the 2010 championship game. Newton led the Tigers down the field, and as time expired, kicker Wes Byrum split the uprights. Auburn completed a 14–0 perfect season and claimed the NCAA title. Coach Gene Chizik was lauded and given a long-term contract that included a $3.5 million annual salary.

Fast forward two years. After a dismal 3–9 record,

Auburn had fallen to the cellar of the Southeastern Conference. It was the worst slide within two years of winning a national championship since 1936, when the Associated Press began its rankings. Someone had to be held accountable. Chizik was fired. Though disappointed, Chizik understood his role. He had been delegated the responsibility to lead his team to success but had fallen far short.[1]

Men, the same holds true in the realm where you have been assigned to rule. God is the ultimate owner. But He has delegated the responsibility to manage your domain, even while He remains sovereign over and within it. You are His representative in good times and in bad. Claim, or reclaim, your authority and lead your team forward.

APPLICATION

1. How successful is your current season?

2. Is there a change you can make to your strategy?

3. What is your game plan for today, this month, and this year?

PRAYER

Lord, give me Your vision and the ability to inspire my team toward it. Amen.

43

A Kingdom Man Is Royal

As soon as he saw Corin and me, it seems
this Centaur looked at me and said, "A day will
come when that boy will save Archenland from
the deadliest danger in which ever she lay."
—Prince Cor, in C. S. Lewis's *The Horse and His Boy*

The message had been delivered to Narnia's King Edmund. The peasant son of the poor Calormen fisherman had done his duty, alerting Narnia and Archenland of the surprise attack. Originally the boy had only intended to escape slavery. But with the help of a talking horse, he had passed through the Calormen palace, across the desert, into an encounter with the mighty Aslan, and over the mountain pass.

But his biggest surprise comes after victory is secured. Shasta is the true heir to the throne of Archenland, the elder of the twin princes Cor and Corin. Shasta, now Cor once again, was kidnapped as an infant. Though he had been raised as a peasant, his true identity is the crown prince.

Men, you are royalty. God has placed a crown on the head of every man and called him majestic. But Satan does not want you to know that you have glory, honor, and dominion. It is time to follow the words of the apostle Paul: "Put on the full armor of God, so that you will be able to stand firm against the schemes of the devil" (Ephesians 6:11). Consider it an act of faith to dress as the royal kingdom man God has created you to be—and to be suited to advance His kingdom against His enemy.

APPLICATION

1. Does your life look like that of a pauper or a prince?

2. What struggle have you mistakenly viewed as against flesh and blood (see Ephesians 6:12)?

3. How will Ephesians 6:10–17 change your outlook and actions today?

PRAYER

God, prepare me for battle, to fight and to lead as a royal in Your service. Amen.

44

A Kingdom Man Seeks God's Plan

Your passion leads you to your purpose, and
both are activated when you put your faith in
your gifts and share them with the world.
—Nick Vujicic, *Unstoppable*

Nick Vujicic (pronounced vooy-cheech) was born with
no limbs. No arms or hands to hold or touch or lift. No
legs to walk or run or move. Besides the physical challenges, the emotional struggle was tremendous. Bullying
was constant. Depression was common. And once ado-
lescence hit, Nick had more than feelings of not fitting
in. He questioned, "Is there anyone on earth *like me?*"[1]

Nick eventually found identity and hope in Christ.
And as he considered what kind of life or career he could
have—or wanted—he discovered a gift of inspiring others through speaking and a passion for sharing the gospel.
Today Nick lives a limitless life in the face of his limitations. He travels the world, speaking to millions as a

living example of God's purpose for each and every life—and the joy of living in it.

God has a plan for you, men. A specific plan. One thing to do to discover that specific plan is to examine your passions, abilities, personality, and experiences, then uncover where those four converge. First Corinthians 12:4 tells us, "Now there are varieties of gifts, but the same Spirit." What passion has God placed inside your heart? What abilities has He gifted your hands? What dreams has He infused in your head? God has given you the authority and ability to accomplish His calling. Follow His lead.

APPLICATION

1. What brings you joy?

2. What are your strengths and weaknesses?

3. Where do you sense God leading you to move beyond false limitations?

PRAYER

God, You have made me for a purpose. Lead and use me according to Your plans. Amen.

45

A Kingdom Man
Gathers Strength

Never fear. EJ is here.

—Ervin "Magic" Johnson, comment to Lakers
coach Paul Westhead before 1980 NBA Finals

The front-row airplane seat belonged to the captain of
the Los Angeles Lakers, and it was empty. Kareem Abdul-
Jabaar, "The Big Man," had been injured the night before
in Game Five of the 1980 NBA Finals. He couldn't even
make this trip to Philadelphia to take the Lakers, three-
games-to-two lead against the 76ers. Boarding the plane
past that empty seat, the Lakers seemed nervous without
their leader. But not Ervin "Magic" Johnson. The twenty-
year-old rookie plopped into the seat and inspired the
team with his confidence.

For the game's tipoff, Johnson lined up for the jump-
ball, then transformed himself into both point guard and
center. At game's end, the Lakers mobbed him to cele-
brate. Johnson had done it all in the NBA's greatest rookie
performance in NBA history: 42 points, 15 rebounds, 7

assists, and 3 steals. Magic Johnson had roared. He had declared his dominion, and he had led his team to an NBA title.[1]

Men, you may be facing uncertainty. You may be nervous from a change or loss. You may lack big-game experience. But you can say, "No fear. *God* is here." He has given you a position of authority under His name— and He will strengthen and equip you to fulfill your role. God has promised, "Do not fear, for I am with you; do not anxiously look about you, for I am your God. I will strengthen you, surely I will help you, surely I will uphold you with My righteous right hand" (Isaiah 41:10). Men, take heart and gather confidence in God's strength. Roar.

APPLICATION

1. What has shaken your confidence?

2. How can you step up today?

3. How will you realize Isaiah 41:10 today?

PRAYER

God, You are my strength. With You, I can. Amen.

46

A Kingdom Man Is Equipped

Now then go, and I, even I, will be with your
mouth, and teach you what you are to say.
—God (Exodus 4:12)

Moses was awed by the bush that burned without being consumed. He was overcome by hearing the voice of God. Yet when he heard God's message, he said, "Who me?" Moses ran through his list of excuses: I'm nobody important. Who should I say sent me? What if they don't believe me? I'm not a good public speaker. God wasn't surprised. He knew what Moses couldn't do—and He knew what He could do through Moses. God answered each doubt. He gave Moses a sign. He gave him the authority of His name, I AM. He gave Moses a tool to use, and He gave him an assistant. God gave Moses everything he needed for the enormous job ahead (Exodus 3–4).

Similarly, God has given you all that you need to rule. If you memorize only one verse in the Bible in your entire life, memorize 2 Corinthians 9:8. The truth of it will blow your mind: "And God is able to make all grace abound to you, so that always having all sufficiency in everything, you may have an abundance for every good deed."

It doesn't matter what opposition you face as a man— it doesn't matter how big the pharaohs are that you face. If you are in the domain where God has placed you, He will give you everything you need to rule with authority to advance His kingdom.

APPLICATION

1. What opposition have you been afraid of?

2. What do you need today that God will supply?

3. How can you walk in the truth of 2 Corinthians 9:8 today?

PRAYER

Heavenly Father, I trust in Your provision and rely on Your sufficiency today. Amen.

A Kingdom Man
Chooses Yes

I will take the Ring to Mordor . . .
though I do not know the way.
—Frodo Baggins, in the movie *The Fellowship of the Ring*

All were gathered at the Council of Elrond, leaders and representatives of every race and nation: elves, dwarves, hobbits, and humans. Evil was mounting its forces, pursuing the ultimate power of the One Ring held by the unassuming hobbit, Frodo Baggins. The destiny of Middle-earth lay in the balance as the Council debated its options.

The Ring must be destroyed, carried into the darkness of Mordor and cast into the fiery chasm of Mount Doom from whence it came. But who could face the utter evil of Sauron's unblinking eye? The council erupted into shouts and arguments until one small voice silenced them all. "I will take it," Frodo said.[1] The smallest and least battle-tested of them all knew what he must do. He didn't know the way. He didn't know exactly how he would accomplish his quest, but Frodo said yes.

Men, you have a choice. God won't force you to rule. He didn't force Moses to lead. Moses could have stayed scared or complacent and walked away saying, "Great locker-room speech, God, but You're just not being realistic." If so, we might read about someone else in the Bible whom God used to set His people free. Instead, Moses eventually said, "I've got it"—just like Frodo said "I've got it"—just like you can say "I've got it."

APPLICATION

1. What is holding you back most from leading: fear, doubt, complacency?

2. How can you shift your focus from your inabilities to God's abilities?

3. Will you take a step of yes today?

PRAYER

Yes, Lord. Amen.

48

A Kingdom Man Sees
with Perspective

> *You come to me with a sword, a spear, and a*
> *javelin, but I come to you in the name of the*
> *LORD of hosts, the God of the armies of Israel,*
> *whom you have taunted . . . The battle is the*
> *LORD'S and He will give you into our hands.*
> —David (1 Samuel 17:45, 47)

Goliath roared and sneered his taunts, and everybody trembled. He was a bully at the top of his game, and while he enjoyed mocking the Israelite army and its God, Goliath was hungry for blood. Problem was, this giant was such a skillful intimidator that no one would step up to challenge him. The men of Israel quaked and quivered before the looming giant.

Yet David saw something different. At half Goliath's size, David had only to look straight ahead to be reminded that Goliath had not been circumcised. Circumcision was a ritual of the covenant between God and

His people. No circumcision meant no covering—God was not on your side. You could be a big and intimidating pagan, but you were still just a pagan. So many men in the Israelite army missed that obvious truth. They looked up at the towering brute and cowered in fear. David didn't look up. He looked straight ahead and said, "I've got it because God's got it." As a result, David accessed God's authority to defeat a giant twice his size.

Men, perspective is never just what you see. Perspective is how you view what you see. Perspective is a key tool in the hands of a kingdom man if he is going to successfully rule.

APPLICATION

1. What is your giant?

2. What do you see differently from another perspective?

3. How will you believe God's victory today?

PRAYER

God, this is Your battle. Open my eyes to see it like You do. Amen.

49

A Kingdom Man
Focuses on Victory

*You're born to be a player. You're meant
to be here. This moment is yours.*

—Coach Herb Brooks, before the US versus
USSR Olympic hockey semifinal, 1980

No one expected much from the US hockey team in the 1980 Olympics. Seeded seventh among twelve teams, the Americans were a bunch of college kids who had recently been crushed 10–3 by the veteran Soviet Union in an exhibition game. Even when the United States surprisingly reached the semifinals against the Soviet Union, the world expected the feel-good story to abruptly end.

The indestructible Soviet hockey machine came out with cold-blooded precision, but the gritty Americans played with relentless confidence. With one second remaining in the first period, the superstar Russian goalkeeper let loose a rebound that American Mark Johnson slid into the net to tie the game. The Soviets were rattled. But they came back strong, pounding shot after shot at the American goal, where goalie Jim Craig made save after save. In the third period, the Americans unbelievably took a one-goal lead, 4–3. With the rink reverberating to chants of "U-S-A!" the Americans completed the "Miracle on Ice," perhaps the greatest underdog victory in sports history. And in the finals they defeated Finland to claim gold medals.[1]

While the world saw a Goliath in the Soviet team, the young Americans kept their focus forward. They played as if they were destined for victory. They played with the covering of their powerful nation. They battled for the outcome they knew was theirs to claim.

Men, never let the size of your giant determine the size of your God.

APPLICATION

1. What challenge seems insurmountable?

2. How have you prepared to overcome it?

3. What Scripture will fuel you toward victory today?

PRAYER

Lord, give me focus on the magnitude of Your power, not the size of my foe. Amen.

50

A Kingdom Man Matters

Carpe diem. Seize the day, boys.
Make your lives extraordinary.
—John Keating, in *Dead Poet's Society*

Ed Stafford went for a walk in April 2008. He finished 860 days later in August 2010. In between he trekked the entire length of the Amazon River, more than four thousand miles. Why? Because no one had ever done it. He wanted to be the first to accomplish an exploratory feat. Was it hard? Absolutely. There were poisonous snakes, stinging insects, jaguars, hostile locals, drug traffickers, and shortages of food, but Ed loved it. He had a mission. He had a goal. There was no way Ed was going to give up. Ed had decided he would not settle for a mediocre existence. He would pursue a great adventure with everything he had.[1]

You have been called to the great adventure of ruling your world and managing your domain. But God never forces you to do so. He has provided you with everything that is necessary to maximize your own life and everyone else's life within your sphere of influence. But far too many men trudge through life—waking up to the same breakfast, heading to the same job, taking the same lunch break, driving home to watch the same television programs—only to wake up the next morning to do it all over again without any passion, zeal, or purpose to see God's kingdom advance through ruling well.

Men, remember, what you do on earth pays forward into how you will be rewarded in eternity. What you do matters. Not just to others. It matters to you.

APPLICATION

1. How would you describe your spiritual passion?

2. What great adventure are you pursuing?

3. What step into the extraordinary is God calling you toward today?

PRAYER

God, shake my heart awake and lead me into Your adventure. Amen.

51

A Kingdom Man Is Free

*The ball happened to be under
the basket. I got it up and stuffed
it in . . . That started it, I guess.*
—Bob Kurland, interview with
the *Orlando Sentinel,* 2012

The game was in Philadelphia in the mid-1940s. The ball was loose. The Oklahoma A&M Aggies big man Bob Kurland picked it and put it in the rim—directly in the rim. It was Kurland's first dunk in a game, but he would repeat the feat again and again. The six-foot, ten-inch center is credited as the first basketball player to dunk the ball regularly. And he was a force to be reckoned with defensively. Kurland made a habit out of swiping opponents' shots out of the air. He was so good at it that the NCAA made a rule in 1945 outlawing goaltending. Yet Kurland was simply a talented player using his skills within the rules of the game. And by doing that he changed basketball.[1]

You have similar freedom. God has turned over the

operation and carrying out of His plan, within prescribed boundaries, to you. The boundary lines around a basketball court give a player the freedom to play. He can maximize those boundaries, even creating new aspects of the game like Kurland did. Within the boundaries God has set around his creation, He wants us to take full advantage of dominion. The primary boundaries involving His will are the two greatest commandments: loving God and loving others. As Paul tells us, "For you were called to freedom, brethren; only do not turn your freedom into an opportunity for the flesh, but through love serve one another" (Galatians 5:13).

Men, play free, and change the game.

APPLICATION

1. What's your latest highlight?

2. What's keeping you on the bench?

3. How can you be a playmaker today?

PRAYER

Father, set me free to love and to lead. Amen.

52

A Kingdom Man
Waits Actively

*It's funny. I could just as easily have
said Our Father or Glory Be.*

—Roger Staubach, to reporters on his famous 1975 "Hail Mary" pass

Is there a more exciting finish than a Super Bowl-winning drive? It's why NFL teams practice the "two-minute drill." While it was Johnny Unitas who invented the two-minute drill in the Greatest Game Ever Played (the 1958 NFL championship that we've already talked about), it was the great Dallas Cowboys quarterback Roger Staubach who coined the phrase *Hail Mary*. Staubach is credited with fifteen fourth-quarter comebacks and twenty-three game-winning drives. In a 1975 playoff game against the Minnesota Vikings, he heaved a fifty-yard desperation pass that Drew Pearson came down with to win. Later, he told reporters, "I just closed my eyes and said a Hail Mary."[1]

Any Hail Mary is a quarterback's only option at the time. It's the step he can take—but he has to take it to win. He can't sit in the huddle hoping or praying for victory. He can't wait for it to come to him. No, he has to call the signals, take the snap, and make the play.

The Bible tells us that at times we are to "Wait for the LORD; be strong and let your heart take courage; yes, wait for the LORD" (Psalm 27:14). But to wait on the Lord does not mean to sit and do nothing. God is waiting on you to take the step of faith or the plan of action that He has given to you. You are waiting on God's means, God's guidance, or God's methods to do it—while you take the step, run the play, and play the game He's put you in.

APPLICATION

1. Have you done your prep by praying?

2. Have you turned to God's Word for guidance?

3. What are you waiting for?

PRAYER

Lord, teach me to wait actively on You: Your means, guidance, and methods. Amen.

53

A Kingdom Man Obeys in Faith

For without risk there is no faith, and the greater the risk, the greater the faith.
Søren Kierkegaard, *Concluding Unscientific Postscript*

One time when I was in seminary, my car started making a lot of noise. All I had left for the month was $50—our tithe. Was I going to trust God's Word and let my actions reflect my faith? Or would I keep the money to fix my car? My $50 went into the offering plate. A couple days later, smoke started pouring out of the hood. After I pulled over, the smoke turned into flames and the front of my car burned up. I had honored God according to how He had instructed me in His Word, and this was how He came through?

At the repair shop, I rushed over and told the mechanic to stop working. I didn't have money for the deductible. That's when he pointed out the fine print on my insurance policy. I didn't have to pay the deductible if my car caught fire. God had waited until I had given Him what He had asked of me, my $50, before meeting my need as He had promised.

Men, God has given us a sphere of influence in which to align our choices and decisions in such a way as to impact others. But often, He will wait to see what we do before revealing what He does, because "Without faith it is impossible to please Him, for he who comes to God must believe that He is and that He is a rewarder of those who seek Him" (Hebrews 11:6).

APPLICATION

1. What step of obedience are you wrestling with?

2. What direction does God's Word give you?

3. What is your decision?

PRAYER

Father, give me the courage to obey and trust. Amen.

54

A Kingdom Man Values His Help

Man's best possession is a sympathetic wife.
—Euripides

A man walked into a flower shop and asked, "What can I get for three dollars?" The proprietor answered, "A dozen carnations or one rose." When the man asked why the difference, the florist said, "Simple: The scent of a carnation doesn't last long. It's sweet for a moment but has no longevity. On the other hand, a rose is known for its ongoing scent. Even when you think it's dead, it can be crushed and turned into fragrant potpourri."[1]

Women are roses. They are valuable. Men, if you view the woman you have married—or will marry if you are single—as simply someone who cooks, cleans your house, wipes noses, and drives the kids to soccer practice, you have not just missed the spiritual component of the nature of a relationship between a man and a woman, you have misused that relationship—to your own detriment. If all you want is someone to do your chores, then hire a maid. Eve was created for much more than that. Eve was created to provide a strong help in the position of counterpart.

Advancing in your destiny is a collaborative effort if you want to advance well. Any man who does not view his mate and look to her skills, insight, intellect, training, and giftedness is a foolish man. Any man who does not encourage her and provide a way for her to sharpen her skills, intellect, and training is an equally foolish man.

APPLICATION

1. Are you treating your wife like a carnation or a rose? Or, how can you prepare to care for a woman tenderly?

2. How much value do your actions and attitudes put on your wife?

3. How can you love your wife today? Or, how can you prepare to be a good husband?

PRAYER

Lord, help me to treat my wife like the valuable treasure, helper, and gift from You that she is. Amen.

55

A Kingdom Man Demonstrates Love

Many waters cannot quench love,
nor will rivers overflow it.
—Song of Solomon 8:7

Three and half years is about the time when married couples start taking each other for granted. A recent survey of married adults found that's when the bad habits take over and couples stop going the extra mile for each other. Among the top signs of marital decay were lack of date nights, forgetting to say I love you daily, going to bed at different times, no longer cuddling on the couch, forgetting to say thank you for dinner, and, yes, breaking wind when your spouse is around.[1]

The less a woman feels appreciated, needed, and valued as equal with you, the less responsive she will be to following your functional lead as the head in your home. To undervalue the woman in your life is one of the gravest mistakes you could ever make. In fact, Peter makes it inextricably clear that a failure to honor her as a fellow heir will actually keep God from responding to your prayers (1 Peter 3:7).

Men, your wife is a gift. Her differences, including the perceptions and intuition of her emotions, complete you as a counterpart. It's your job to set the emotional temperature in the home, to cover and nurture and love as Christ loves the church. Remember the days of your early love—and live and lead daily in ways that remind your wife of them too.

APPLICATION

1. When did you fall in love with your wife? Or, if you're not married, how will you show love to the woman you intend to marry?

2. What bad relational habits do you need to break? If you're not married, how can you equip yourself to be a loving husband in the future?

3. How will you rekindle romance today?

PRAYER

Father, refuel the fires of romance (or prepare me for future romance) and deepen our marriage. Amen.

56

A Kingdom Man Blesses

You don't pay love back; you pay it forward.
—Lily Hardy Hammond, *In the Garden of Delight*

Most cities have food banks and blood banks. Although these banks are set up to collect, they are not designed simply to hoard and to store. The resources they gather help other people to live—either by the infusion of food or by the infusion of nutrients from blood. That's the same way blessing works. God has saved and blessed Christians so that we can share those blessings with others.

A blessing isn't simply more stuff or more money. A blessing isn't merely getting everything you think you might want. A blessing is never only about you. It includes you, but it is intended to go through you to others.

When God blessed Adam and Eve in the garden, He told them to be fruitful and multiply. Then He enabled them to fill the earth and extend the blessing He had given them throughout the land. Another way that God blessed them was that He provided resources in the place where they were supposed to rule. A blessing is when God supplies you for your calling. It is when God provides all that is needed for you to accomplish all that is under your rule. You know that you have been blessed when you're able to enjoy the goodness of God despite the trials and tribulations associated with what you're doing. And you have access to enough strength, assets, and capacity to do what you have been called to do to bless others.

APPLICATION

1. What recent blessings have you received?

2. What blessing have you held too tightly?

3. How can you bless someone else today?

PRAYER

God, thank Your for all You have given to me. Help me to pass it on. Amen.

57

A Kingdom Man
Names God's Work

Now faith is the assurance of things hoped
for, the conviction of things not seen.
—Hebrews 11:1

Years ago God had put it on my heart that a particular vacant, run-down building was going to be used for His glory. So I pulled my car up in front of it and said, "God, I name that. I name this entire place for the good of others and for your glory. We don't have the money for it right now, but God, hold it for us. Because I name it in Jesus' name." Not too long after that day, God revealed a way for us to get it. And now on that land and in that building is a pregnancy center where the message of restoration and new beginnings is given to teen girls in crisis every day.

I now go throughout my day looking for something I can name. Then I watch in anticipation for God to bring it to fruition. Naming—like everything a man is supposed to do—is always tied to God's glory and the expansion of His kingdom. It is assigning divine involvement based on how God's revealed will and Word says He will be involved. It requires an intimate and abiding relationship with God so you are attuned to what He is bringing to you.

When you get the opportunity to name things and watch God bring them into being, it means that even God is respecting your manhood. God is free to respect your manhood when you respect His Godhood. That's how you experience kingdom success. And nothing is quite like seeing God open doors that have been slammed shut.

APPLICATION

1. What truth has God been revealing to you in His Word?

2. What do you sense God has in store?

3. What work do you want to see Him accomplish?

PRAYER

Lord, increase my faith; fill me with expectation; use me to name and realize Your work. Amen.

58

A Kingdom Man Has a Calling to Name

Remember, with great power
comes great responsibility.
—Uncle Ben, in *Spider-Man*

A name is never just a word. A name is a revelation and an expectation. And the Bible is filled with examples of God changing the names of His followers. Abram became Abraham, "the father of a multitude of nations" (Genesis 17:5). Sarai became Sarah, "princess" (Genesis 17:15). Jacob became Israel, "he who strives with God" (Genesis 32:28). Simon became Cephas, or Peter, "rock" (John 1:42). Each name change was a symbol of God's reality and identity; it was a spoken expression of who these individuals were and how God was using them. It encapsulated themes of function and purpose.

Before naming comes calling. A kingdom man's ability to name must be rooted in the authority that God has given him. With that authority to name come influence and power—something most men gravitate toward—but authority also comes with responsibility. A kingdom man who aligns himself under the lordship of Jesus Christ will be accountable for all that composes his role. God named Adam. Adam named Eve, demonstrating the flow of accountability and responsibility. God authorizes dominion only when a man functions as a subordinate to Him and the governance He gives. If a man is trying to do his own thing, or promote his own agenda in his own kingdom, he will lack the authority to name.

Men, call into being that which will further God's kingdom.

APPLICATION

1. What name is God giving you?

2. What calling has God given you?

3. How can you walk with authority today?

PRAYER

Father, let me live Your reality, bearing Your name with wisdom and strength. Amen.

59

A Kingdom Man Knows True Success

It's not so important who starts
the game but who finishes it.

—John Wooden, quoted in *Coach Wooden: The 7 Principles
that Shaped His Life and Will Change Yours*

A trip to Super Bowl XLVI was on the line in the NFC
Championship game between the San Francisco 49ers
and the New York Giants. With the game tied 17–17
in overtime, the Giants were forced to punt. The 49ers
Kyle Williams made the catch but fumbled the ball on
the return. Devin Thomas pounced on the ball to recover
it for the Giants. The rare turnover for the 49ers was a
costly one. Five plays later, the Giants scored the game-
winning field goal.[1]

A fumble can be a critical error—or a game-changing
success, depending on which team you're on. Adam
fumbled the ball in the garden. And at that moment, the
kingdom of darkness ruled by Satan issued a challenge to

the kingdom of light ruled by God. Yet what Adam lost in the garden, Christ regained at the cross. He won the victory and secured your success.

Your success means fulfilling your destiny. This kingdom success runs much deeper than the width of a wallet, the square footage of a home, or the smiles in a photograph hanging on a wall. Success has to do with fulfilling the reason why you were both born and born again. It involves living out your ordained reason for being—for God's glory, your good, and the benefit of others.

Men, scoop up that fumble and run it into the end zone.

APPLICATION

1. What definition of success have you been pursuing?

2. How will you recover a fumble?

3. How will you keep a positive momentum going today?

PRAYER

Lord, keep my eyes on Your victory and my hands on the ball. Amen.

60

A Kingdom Man
Sees True Victory

When you win, nothing hurts.
—Joe Namath

Sweat trickles down your forehead. You feel your pulse throb in your temples as you try to slow your breathing. You know the enemy is out there. You've caught glimpses through your infrared goggles. Are you stalking him or is he stalking you? Suddenly you catch a blur in your peripheral vision—a flash of fire. A crack breaks the silence. Instinctively you duck for cover and roll to return fire. You discharge several rounds when you feel a sharp sting. You've been hit! As you turn to assess the damage, you spot the seep of red vivid on your chest. Good thing it's only a paintball.

Men, you have a real enemy, but his authority is limited. Not only is Jesus Christ the "head over all rule and authority," but He has also "disarmed the rulers and authorities . . . having triumphed over them through Him"

(Colossians 2:10, 15). When Christ disarmed Satan, He removed the authority Satan had gained in the garden over humankind. Satan still has power, but he has no authority. There's a big difference between those two, just as there is a big difference between someone standing in front of you holding a real, loaded gun and someone standing in front of you holding a paintball gun.

The truth is that Satan's gun is empty. With Christ's death on the cross, God removed the bullets and "rescued us from the domain of darkness and transferred us to the kingdom of His beloved Son" (Colossians 1:13). Victory is yours.

APPLICATION

1. Are you living like your enemy's gun is loaded or empty?

2. Are your eyes on your Victor or your enemy?

3. How will you step into victory today?

PRAYER

Lord, give me God-vision goggles to see the enemy as You do. Amen.

61

A Kingdom Man Plays with Confidence

Anything to get the Red Sox out
would be awesome for me.

—Russell Martin, New York Yankees catcher,
to reporters on September 22, 2011

By the end of the 2012 season, the Boston Red Sox had only one thing left to play for: spoiling the New York Yankees chances of making the play-offs. The two teams hold arguably the biggest rivalry in all of sports. The hatred spans more than a century. The teams have squared off more than 2,100 times since 1901. And if one can't win championships, the next best thing is to make sure the other loses too. The Red Sox were out of contention early in 2012, but with six games between them in the final month, the Sox had a shot at barring the Yankees from the postseason too. Ultimately, the Yankees prevailed, but the Sox found a renewed reason to play.[1]

Likewise, Satan's goal is to rob us of our spiritual

"championship bid" and drag us down to his level. Satan knows that God has "blessed us with every spiritual blessing in the heavenly places in Christ" (Ephesians 1:3), but he's committed to keeping us from reaching our destiny.

But you are a subject in God's kingdom, so Satan no longer has legal authority over you. You don't need to live playing defense or being afraid. Jesus has declared that all authority has been given to Him, and in Him, you have been made complete. You are seated with Him where He rules in the heavenly places. Stay in alignment under the headship of Christ, men, and you will have access to all the power you need to do all that God has destined you to do.

APPLICATION

1. Are you playing scared or with confidence?

2. Have you been surrendering power to your opponent?

3. How will you execute God's game plan today?

PRAYER

Father, help me to live like Your victor. Amen.

62

A Kingdom Man Prays from the Heart

To pray is to work, to work is to pray.
—Ancient motto of the Benedictine order

Going through college and seminary while married with children had taken a toll on our finances. My wife, Lois, believed God's call on my life, but the burden had grown too great. Knowing that my primary responsibility under God as a man was to meet the emotional, physical, and spiritual needs of my family first, I told Lois I would drop out of seminary to get a full-time job. But I asked, "What would it take for you to receive today in order for you to support me continuing in seminary and not dropping out?" She thought about it and said, "Five hundred dollars." That was a lot of money in the 1970s! You better believe I prayed. After classes, I opened my mailbox and saw five one-hundred-dollar bills attached to a note from a man named John who said that God had told him to give this to me today.

Prayer is the most underused tool in the arsenal of a kingdom man. The secret in praying is not necessarily in how long you pray or what kind of fancy words you pray; it's in discovering God's will for your life and then asking for it. When you find out what God wants, what His heart is about, then your prayers will line up with Him. If His words are abiding in you, His wishes will become your wishes, and He will "give you the desires of your heart" (Psalm 37:4), because your desires will be His desires.

Prayer involves knowing God, listening to Him, and aligning your heart with His. When a kingdom man is properly aligned, his prayers will get answered.

APPLICATION

1. How are you praying?

2. What answers have you received to your prayers?

3. What is your prayer today?

PRAYER

God, let's talk . . .

63

A Kingdom Man Wrestles with God

I don't think I've ever been so ready to wrestle.
—Wrestler Rulon Gardner, Olympic gold-medal winner, 2000

Alexander Karelin was unbeatable. Known as the "Russian Bear" and "Alexander the Great," Karelin had never lost in fifteen years of international Greco-Roman wrestling—hadn't even surrendered a single point! He had won three Olympic gold medals and seven world titles. The mountain of muscle was understandably feared. It was no surprise he was in the gold-medal match at the 2000 Olympics. American Rulon Gardner, on the other hand, never won even an NCAA title while at the University of Nebraska. That's why it was such a shocker when Gardner emerged victorious, matching every attack from Karelin, gaining confidence, and besting the one-man dynasty.[1]

Like Jacob who wrestled with God all night until he got a response from heaven, men are to wrestle with God until heaven responds. What God says He wants to do doesn't always happen on Earth just because He declared it to be. Often, God is waiting on our labor to bring it down. This is because He has given dominion to man. Prayer is the human means of entering the supernatural realm to have heaven visit Earth. The invisible gets pulled down through prayer.

Men, exercise your power in prayer. Persevere. "Pray without ceasing" (1 Thessalonians 5:17). Pray according to God's Word, asking for what He has already said will happen.

Application

1. Do you believe while you pray?

2. What prayer needs have you given up on?

3. What Scripture verse will you pray today?

Prayer

Lord, I bring You my needs again in faith You will answer and move in my life. Amen.

64

A Kingdom Man
Reaches into Heaven

Pray often, for prayer is a shield to the soul,
a sacrifice to God, and a scourge for Satan.
—John Bunyan, *Mr. John Bunyan's Dying Sayings*

The lead changed six times in the NFC Championship on January 10, 1982. The mighty Dallas Cowboys were ahead 27–21 when the San Francisco 49ers got the ball back with 4:54 left to play.

Imagine this: Joe Montana drives the team downfield to the Dallas 6-yard line. The snap comes with fifty-eight seconds left. Montana rolls right almost to the sideline. With three Cowboys closing in, he jumps and throws. The ball floats high. It looks like it will sail out of the back of the end zone. But Dwight Clark leaps across, his six-foot-four body fully extended, and grabs the ball in his fingertips. Touchdown 49ers! The extra point secures the win and brings an end to the Cowboys' dominant

NFC dynasty. "The Catch" lives on as one of the all-time greatest.[1]

Men, you are in a war. You are in a spiritual conflict. Others have lined up to face you, and their only goal is to keep you from advancing God's kingdom down the field of life. Because of them, the passes thrown to you can't always be within your grasp. In fact, often because of the nature of the battle, they are thrown high. Yet you have been given all that you need to reach up into heaven and bring victory down to earth. Prayer is a kingdom man's primary weapon of warfare. With it, you will touch heaven and change earth.

APPLICATION

1. What is waiting at your fingertips?

2. What will you ask, seek, and knock for (Matthew 7:7)?

3. What pass is yours to receive from God today?

PRAYER

God, give me the courage to reach into heaven and bring your victory to earth. Amen.

65

A Kingdom Man
Plugs Into Power

The LORD is my strength and my
shield; my heart trusts in Him.
—Psalm 28:7

Telephone technology has come a long way. Do you remember the first models of cordless or car phones? The handsets were as big as battlefield walkie-talkies, and they couldn't go far from their large base units without losing connection. But they were high tech compared to phones that were connected by cords to walls or desks. Now our pocket-size smartphones will go almost anywhere—until you hear that beeping and buzzing and your battery runs out. Even our amazing cell phones need to be plugged into their power source. They can stay away only so long without becoming nonfunctional. Once we plug them back in, we can hear and communicate and access all the apps that make us effective once again.

Men, God has fully supplied all that you need to

exercise the authority He has given to you. Yet God is not going to force that authority and power on you. God's Word tells us, "Be strong in the Lord and in his mighty power" (Ephesians 6:10, NIV). He is our power source, but we've got to plug ourselves in on an ongoing basis. Too many men are waiting on God to move in regard to their personal problems, issues, or challenges, or in regard to their families, careers, or vision, yet God has already supplied all that is needed for them to rule. He is waiting on them to walk only in His ways so that He can charge them with His power. It's time to do something with the authority Christ has given you.

APPLICATION

1. How is your battery power?

2. Are you recharging regularly?

3. How will you draw and use God's power today?

PRAYER

Father, you are my Source of strength. Guide me in using it today. Amen.

66

A Kingdom Man Leaves the Past Behind

> *My mama always said you've got to put the*
> *past behind you before you can move on.*
> —Forrest Gump, in the motion picture *Forrest Gump*

Karl Benz built the first car powered by an internal combustion engine in 1885. Fifteen years later, his company was the largest manufacturer of automobiles. Drivers of those early cars wore goggles to protect their eyes, but nothing stopped bugs from flying in their mouths until the windshields were introduced in 1904.[1]

Do you know why a car's windshield is bigger than its rearview mirror? Because where you're going is a lot more important than where you've been. The apostle Paul knew this fact. He had a regrettable past, but through Jesus Christ his future was glorious. In Philippians 3:13–14, Paul writes, "Forgetting what *lies* behind and reaching forward to what *lies* ahead, I press on toward the goal for the prize of the upward call of God in Christ Jesus."

All of us have pasts that involve the good, the bad, and the ugly. But that was yesterday. That was the past. Whenever I go back to Baltimore to visit my parents, I inevitably run into some guys whom I knew growing up. These men are still on the same corner talking the same noise that we used to talk as teenagers. The topic that dominates every discussion continues to be *yesterday.*

I'm not saying yesterday is a bad conversation topic, but you don't want to get stuck there. Yesterday's victories will not carry you through today. Yesterday's defeats should not dominate tomorrow. Remember, if Satan can keep you looking back, then he can keep you from moving forward.

APPLICATION

1. Do you have any friends stuck in their glory days? How does talking to them make you feel?

2. Do you think God cares more about your past or your future?

3. What can you do to help yourself move forward?

PRAYER

Father, help me to forget my past and strive to move forward. Amen.

67

A Kingdom Man Walks in Faith

For we walk by faith, not by sight.

—2 Corinthians 5:7

In Jesus's first recorded miracle, He turned water into wine at a marriage ceremony. During Bible times, wine making was a slow, arduous process. Grapes were piled into a large basin where men would step on them to squeeze out the juice. Often four men stomped on the grapes in the wine press, while holding onto ropes that helped support their weight. The juice from the grapes ran into collection tubs. Then the juice was fermented and turned into wine.[1]

The Hebrew word *darak* refers to "a press." It's the word used to describe treading on grapes, and it's the same word used in Joshua 1:3 when the Lord says, "Every place on which the sole of your foot treads, I have given it to you."[2] When a kingdom man treads upon that which God has destined for him, he is not trying to get God to give him something. He is simply walking on that which

God has already provided. He is squeezing out the goodness of God's promises.

God has an inheritance and destiny for you. But one reason why you may not have experienced it yet is because your feet have not marched in tune with faith. Faith means you believe God so much that you are going to act on what He says. Faith is when you act as if God is telling the truth. And God *always* tells the truth. God *is* the waymaker. He *is* our provider. He *does* miracles. And just as at the wedding ceremony, He often saves the best for last.

APPLICATION

1. How can you show more faith in God's promises?

2. Where do you feel God is telling you to step out in faith?

3. Is faith more of an action or a belief?

PRAYER

Lord, I desire the inheritance and destiny that You have for me. Help me to put feet to my faith. Amen.

68

A Kingdom Man Seizes His Inheritance

Nothing happens until something moves.
—Albert Einstein

She finally put two and two together. Well, really, much more than that. A California woman finally discovered that she had stashed a lottery ticket in her glove compartment—a winning lottery ticket. While it was gathering dust, the California Lottery was searching for the winner of twenty-three million dollars. When five months had passed without hearing from anyone, lottery officials posted a surveillance photo of the woman who had bought it earlier in 2012. The ticket would expire in twenty-five days. That prize belonged to someone, but she had to step up and claim it. She did indeed after seeing her picture. But can you imagine what her reaction would have been if she'd learned her winning ticket had expired?[1]

Men, you hold a prize far more valuable than a winning lottery ticket. But you must seize your inheritance. Everything that God has destined for you, He has already given to you. Paul said, "Blessed be the God and Father of our Lord Jesus Christ, who has blessed us with every spiritual blessing in the heavenly places in Christ" (Ephesians 1:3). Your job is to draw it down. What God says in the invisible spiritual realm gets pulled down through faith. God is the Way-maker. He is our Provider. He does miracles. But most of the time, God works through the ordinary act of obeying whatever He has said to do.

Faith means that you believe God so much that you are going to act on what He says. Faith is never simply a feeling. Faith always involves movement. Get moving.

APPLICATION

1. What spiritual prize are you letting go unclaimed?

2. What does Ephesians 1:3 mean to your life?

3. How will you move in faith today?

PRAYER

Lord, open my eyes as I step out in obedience to You. Amen.

69

A Kingdom Man Defeats Giants

They don't measure heart by inches. They
don't measure courage. . . . I tip my hat to
their courage and to their conviction.

—University of Connecticut coach Jim Calhoun
after losing to George Mason in 2006 Elite Eight

Everybody loves an underdog story. Millions watch every March to see which little-known school will become a giant killer in the annual NCAA men's basketball tournament. In 2006 the underdog was eleventh-seeded George Mason. The Patriots had lost in the Colonial Athletic Associate tournament, and many felt their season was over. It wasn't.

George Mason drew basketball powerhouse Michigan State in the first round. With their tallest player standing six-feet-seven inches, the Patriots were outsized by several inches at every position. But they beat the Spartans. They defeated North Carolina and Wichita State too, setting up a matchup against Connecticut in the

Elite Eight. George Mason toppled that giant as well to advance all the way to the Final Four. [1]

At times in your life, you'll feel like an underdog. You'll face giants that seem impossible to overcome. Remember that people, on their best day, are still just people. And God is still God. God's power can bring down any giant, but we have to be willing to get in the game. That doesn't mean to disrespect or dishonor people; it just means you do not need to be intimidated by them. While your opposition may have a say, he does not have the final say. God does. One of the greatest experiences that you can have is watching God override people, especially people who you thought could not be overridden.

APPLICATION

1. Who are the giants you're facing?

2. In what areas of your life do you think God wants you to show more faith?

3. When did you have to overcome a giant? How did it feel?

PRAYER

God, you are much bigger than any challenge I face. Make me fearless through Your power. Amen.

70

A Kingdom Man
Follows God's Leading

One of the Bible's greatest truths is that
God actually wants to guide us.
—Billy Graham, "Billy Graham's *My Answer*," August 16, 2012

Years ago evangelist Billy Graham received a letter asking him how to successfully follow God's leading. After first telling the letter writer to memorize Proverbs 3:5–6, Graham wrote, "The first step in seeking God's guidance is to be sure we actually want it. All too often, we want God to bless our plans, instead of asking Him what His plans are."[1]

A kingdom man puts God's plans ahead of his own. He actively seeks God's guidance. Living a successful life as a child of the King is not rocket science. God doesn't hide the path toward living out your destiny in some well-guarded vault in the Cayman Islands. Seeking the will of God boils down to following the ways of the King. The more God is the Ruler of your life, the more you will see Him opening doors. And you will know that it is God opening the doors because He will do things that you didn't even know He was going to do. God's precepts and principles are predictable; His ways are unpredictable, which is why God says, "So are My ways higher than your ways, and My thoughts than your thoughts" (Isaiah 55:9).

By abiding in an intimate relationship with God through His Word, the Holy Spirit will give and confirm God's leading in your life. And when you are certain of His leading, go do it! I wish I could shout from the top of the highest mountaintop, "Get up, men. Stop whining. Stop blaming. Stop fearing. Get up and get what God has for you."

APPLICATION

1. Do you follow your plans more often than God's plans?

2. How can you better follow God's leading in your life?

3. What would you shout to other men around you?

PRAYER

God, I want to be successful in following Your leading. Amen.

71

A Kingdom Man Has a Vision

The soul never thinks without an image.
—Aristotle, *De Anima, Book III*

In 1878 a father brought a surprise toy home to his boys. Before he even showed them what it was, he tossed it into the air. Instead of falling, it flew across the room. It was known to scientists as a helicoptère. It sparked a vision within the boys, a vision that eventually led Orville and Wilbur Wright to fly. It guided their curiosity, their dreams, their pursuit, and their passion. Orville said, "If birds can glide for long periods of time, then . . . why can't I?" The thought captivated and guided them until 1903 when the Wright brothers soared from the top of Kill Devil Hill near Kitty Hawk, North Carolina, and into history.[1]

Men, you need a vision to guide you in aligning every area of life with God's kingdom agenda. Psalm 128 lays out that vision. It has become my benchmark passage for manhood. In this psalm, David outlines the life of a kingdom man. He begins with the personal life of a man who fears the Lord: "How blessed is everyone who fears the LORD, who walks in His ways" (Psalm 128:1). Then he moves to family life, church life, and community life, including his greater society and his legacy.

Men, read this psalm, study it, and let it shape your vision for living as a kingdom man. This is your mantra.

APPLICATION

1. What is your guiding vision?

2. How does Psalm 128 shape your life?

3. How will you apply it today?

PRAYER

Lord, be and guide my vision. Amen.

72

A Kingdom Man Prays

I pray because the need flows out of
me all the time, waking and sleeping.
It doesn't change God; it changes me.
—C. S. Lewis, in *Shadowlands*

The average man has a constant flurry of voices competing for his attention, due in part to all the devices we carry around. We get cell calls, texts, emails, tweets, social media updates . . . oh, and the *commercials!* Did you know you're hit with approximately 5,000 ads daily?[1] To escape all that nattering, we run music through our earbuds, listen to talk radio or pull up a favorite app. As a result, the Lord's "gentle whisper" (1 Kings 19:12) has its work cut out for it in a world uncomfortable with silence.

That's why a kingdom man needs to be more intentional than ever about spending time with God in prayer. *Time.* As busy as we are, that can be a scary word. But the apostle Paul told the Thessalonians to "pray continually" (1 Thessalonians 5:17), because he realized that communicating with God is an ebbing, flowing joint venture that brings heaven into history. And a man on his knees is a menacing warrior.

Sometimes as a boy, I would wake up around midnight and go downstairs to check out a noise I'd heard. It would be my father on his knees praying fervently for our family. He was never too tired. Never too busy. The time he spent at the throne of God made all the difference in our lives, and it will do the same for you.

APPLICATION

1. Are you more inclined to work for God or talk to God? Why?

2. Who should you be praying for right now?

3. How can you silence some of the noise drowning out God's voice?

PRAYER

Almighty God, give me ears to hear Your voice and the discipline to maintain an ongoing, honest dialogue with You. Amen.

73

A Kingdom Man Is a Blessing

The evidence never lies.
—Gil Grissom, in *CSI: Crime Scene Investigation*

You can't channel surf without running into a TV show about crime scene investigators. These forensic scientists study evidence to answer numerous questions, including "Who was here?" By studying the aftermath of an event, investigators can learn more about the person who committed the crime. But it's not just the bad guys who leave behind evidence of their activities. When a kingdom man blesses others, there are always telltale signs that he's been there.

As you seek blessings in your own life, it's important to remember that any blessings you receive are intended to pass *through* you and touch other people. Our benevolent God wants you to be a conduit, not a cul-de-sac. An answered prayer or met need shouldn't be the end of things. Rather, let it become one link in a chain of blessing. In fact, when you pray, take time to consider how God's response to that petition could also benefit someone else. Make it a habit that once you've received a blessing, you'll *be* a blessing.

The evidence never lies. As investigators study the scene of a blessing, they'll learn more about your role in it and, ultimately, the One behind it. As Jesus said in Matthew 5:16, "Let your light shine before men, that they may see your good deeds and praise your Father in heaven."

APPLICATION

1. How has the Lord blessed you?

2. How has God used you to be a blessing to others?

3. Why is it important to credit Him when we bless people?

PRAYER

Heavenly Father, make me unselfish as I approach you, always looking for opportunities to meet others' needs in addition to my own. Amen.

74

A Kingdom Man Fears the Lord

The fear of the LORD is the beginning of wisdom
—Psalm 111:10

The National Institute of Mental Health says that 19.2 million American adults struggle with some sort of phobia.[1] Of course, in our society fear is something to be conquered at all costs. Our culture tells us a real man isn't afraid of anything. When fear starts to creep in, we men try to exterminate it. We blast it with everything we've got. But Psalm 111:10 tells us that "the fear of the LORD is the beginning of wisdom." So clearly, all fears are not unhealthy.

The Hebrew word for fear in this case is *yare*.[2] It combines the concepts of dread and awe. In conjunction, it implies coming under God's authority and holding Him in the highest esteem, taking Him seriously rather than casually. It's an attitude. Is the Lord our friend? Absolutely, but there's a difference between having intimate fellowship with our heavenly Father and treating the holy, righteous God of the universe like a chum. A healthy fear of the Lord keeps us from forgetting who we are and who He is.

To be a kingdom man and experience blessings in your life, you must possess a reverent dread and awe of the One who made you . . . and loves you. It should affect your thoughts and actions when no one but God is watching. Call it fear. Call it a phobia. The Bible calls it the beginning of wisdom.

APPLICATION

1. What are you afraid of? How is that different from a healthy fear of God?

2. When have you found yourself taking too casual an attitude toward God?

3. How should a Christian approach the Lord?

PRAYER

Lord, open my eyes to all that You are. Help me to embrace You as a friend without losing sight of Your holiness. Amen.

75

A Kingdom Man
Gives God His Best

*There is always some kid who may be seeing
me for the first time. I owe him my best.*
—Joe Dimaggio

When you buy a ticket to a sporting event, you'd like to think the players intend to give it their all. But that's not always the case. In recent years, some athletes have even admitted that they pace themselves and, while on the field, take a night off now and then. When can we expect to see pro-athletes play their best? In a *contract year*. What a terrible attitude! As much as athletes depend on fan support, the fans deserve more respect.

Sadly, we can dishonor God much the same way. For example, in the days of the prophet Malachi, God scolded the Israelites for calling Him Father and Master, yet failing to show Him proper respect at the altar. God deserved their best offerings, but priests had been sacrificing animals that were lame, sick, or blind. That's not much of a sacrifice. And God's people had the audacity to expect a blessing in return for this half-hearted effort.

Is your heavenly Father getting your best, or is He being forced to settle for leftovers? Leftover time. Leftover service. Leftover money. You don't need to curse God to despise Him (Malachi 1:6–9). Just tell Him you don't think much of Him by holding back your very best. It may be a long season, but a kingdom man doesn't take nights off.

APPLICATION

1. Who deserves your best? Why?

2. In what way might you be giving God leftovers?

3. In what everyday ways can you show respect to others or to God?

PRAYER

Father, forgive me for expecting Your blessing while giving You less of my time, service, and resources than You deserve. Amen.

76

A Kingdom Man Denies Himself

Alas, this time is never the time for self-denial, it is always the next time.
—George MacDonald, *Sir Gibbie*

When was the last time you told yourself, "No"? Did you squelch a temptation, ignore an appetite, or put a counterproductive urge in its place? If so, congratulations! That's a discipline every kingdom man needs to cultivate. After all, when Jesus commissioned His disciples, He made it clear they wouldn't be sashaying down the path of least resistance. Quite the opposite. In Matthew 16:24 He noted, "If anyone wishes to come after Me, he must deny himself, take up his cross and follow Me."

Self-denial doesn't come naturally. That's because your biggest problem isn't outside of you; it's inside of you. More to the point, your biggest problem *is* you. I like fried chicken so much I almost missed an airplane flight because I didn't want to leave the too-hot-to-eat chicken behind. It took all that I had to say no to my-self and board the plane (taking the chicken with me!). I need more than willpower to resist eating too much fried chicken. I have developed good eating habits, and I let God work in me so that I'm no longer a slave to my cravings.[1]

When a believer denies himself and carries his cross, he is submitting to another law higher than himself. He exchanges his own wants and desires for those of the One he has chosen to follow. Even Jesus wrestled with this tension before going to the cross (Luke 22:42–44). Self-denial is a daily discipline, but the rewards are worth it.

APPLICATION

1. When is it hardest to tell yourself no?

2. What steps can you take to make strides in this area?

3. Whom can you be accountable to?

PRAYER

Dear God, make my desires Your desires. Let me see things as You do so that following You comes more and more naturally. Amen.

77

A Kingdom Man Sharpens Others

*As iron sharpens iron, so one
man sharpens another.*
—Proverbs 27:17

A successful husband and father not only brings blessing into his own life, but he also enables those around him to fulfill their divine destinies. In a way, he's like El Afilador de Cuchillos, the humble knife sharpener who rides through the streets of Mexico City on his bicycle, blowing a whistle that tells the locals he's passing through. People bring out their cutlery, blades, and ax heads. He puts the rear wheel of his bike on a stand, then peddles backward to spin the sharpening stone. Because of his presence, everyone returns to work sharper and more efficient.[1]

Empowering others to succeed begins at home. God designed the covenant of marriage to increase the capacity of both partners to carry out their purpose for advancing His kingdom. If your wife is going to fulfill her divine destiny, you need to provide a secure, stable, and spiritually strong environment that will keep her sharp.

Likewise, your children need your help to become all the Lord intended them to be. The purpose of children isn't merely to have look-alikes in your ancestral line, but to produce image-bearers of God who will reflect His character as they change the world for Jesus.

An insecure man frustrates and controls those around him. A kingdom man puts them in a position to succeed, often at his own expense. Climb on your bike and start peddling!

APPLICATION

1. How has God gifted you to sharpen others?

2. Ask your wife, "What can I do to help you fulfill your calling?"

3. When have you equipped someone to achieve greatness?

PRAYER

Father, help me to focus on my family's gifts and divine purpose, and guide my attempts to make everyone around me stronger. Amen.

78

A Kingdom Man Defends the Family

But as for me and my household,
we will serve the LORD.
—Joshua 24:15

At seven-foot-two and 260 pounds, legendary NBA shot-blocker Dikembe Mutombo was an imposing presence in the paint. The man knew how to play defense. He lined up at center for six pro teams following a stellar career at Georgetown, where he averaged 4.71 rejections per game his senior year.[1] In 2013, a GEICO commercial further immortalized Mutombo's skills by showing him swatting away everyday objects tossed by everyday people, wagging his finger and saying, "Not in my house!"[2]

As a kingdom man, you'll need to do a little "rejecting," too. Our world has its own flawed ideas about what a husband and father should look like, and they're wreaking havoc in millions of homes. If Satan can destroy the institution of the family, he can destroy the expansion of God's kingdom rule. That's a key part of the devil's game plan.

He wants to weaken the family unit. He wants to redefine it. That starts by twisting your priorities and warping your view of manhood. Like an all-star shot-blocker—or Joshua addressing the tribes of Israel at Shechem—it's time to declare what will or won't happen in your house.

Family must come first after God. It's how He designed our lives to function. And when we operate according to the principles of His covenantal and transcendent rule, not only are we blessed, but those within our realm find themselves fruitful and blessed as they become what they were destined to be.

APPLICATION

1. What false ideas about manhood and family have you rejected?

2. How is your leadership inspiring your household to serve the Lord?

3. How is Satan undermining the family today? What can you do to stand in the gap?

PRAYER

Lord, teach me to know Your will for my household and to defend the institution You have established to expand Your rule in history. Amen.

79

A Kingdom Man
Doesn't Turn Back

Marriage is the only adventure
open to the cowardly.
—Voltaire

According to legend, Spanish Conquistador Hernando Cortes arrived on the shores of Mexico to conquer the Aztecs in 1519, and then he promptly ordered his men to burn the ships that brought them there. They faced long odds, and Cortes knew they might be tempted to turn back if times got hard. So he eliminated that option. Within two years, his small, totally committed army had won the victory.[1]

A kingdom man needs to approach marriage the same way. Once you set sail on the seas of matrimony, as far as God is concerned there's no turning back. You have entered into a *covenant*. That's not some flimsy contract you can dissolve when passion fades or if you decide you'd be happier someplace else. In Scripture, it's a spiritually binding relationship based on a divinely authored promise. Too many couples embark on marriage as a romantic adventure only to quit when the going gets tough.

The level of commitment in your marriage forms the bedrock of your family. How strong is it? Are you reaping the blessings of a covenant relationship, or are you feeling insecure about the future because, emotionally, you've left your options open? Burn the ships. Marriage isn't always easy, but if men trust God for the victory and refuse to turn back, they will create a legacy of honor sure to impact generations to come.

APPLICATION

1. Why are feelings a poor barometer for marital success?

2. How are unmet needs and unfulfilled expectations Satan's foothold?

3. If you're married, what can you do to reassure your wife of your commitment? If you're not, how can you prepare to be a kingdom husband?

PRAYER

Dear God, help me to see my marriage as a symbol of the new covenant You've made with Your people, and to honor it as such. Amen.

80

A Kingdom Man Lays It All Down

[Sacrifice is] not something you regret.
It's something you aspire to.
—Mitch Albom, *The Five People You Meet in Heaven*

Thirty-three-year-old Brian Wood was driving home when his Subaru Outback was struck by an oncoming Chevy Blazer. His wife, Erin, was in the passenger seat. "Wood swerved his car and put himself directly in the path of the oncoming SUV," one news report said. It was a "decision that ultimately cost him his life, but protected his wife and unborn child from harm."[1]

Brian Wood's choice is a tragic but vivid illustration of what the apostle Paul tells men in Ephesians 5:25: "Husbands, love your wives, just as Christ also loved the church and gave himself up for her." I pray none of you has to make a life-or-death sacrifice like that. But how to choose to treat your wife daily can have as much impact.

As a kingdom husband, I have many responsibilities to the woman I love within our spiritually binding covenant relationship. I am to provide for her. I am to pastor her. I'm to meet her emotional and physical needs. But most of all, I must be her "savior" if I'm going to love her the way Christ loved the church. That means selflessly putting my life on the line for her well-being in small ways every single day.

Biblical love isn't about feelings. It's about humbly and passionately pursuing the well-being of our wives, even if that comes at great personal cost.

APPLICATION

1. Do most men see marriage as a non-binding contract or a sacred covenant? How about you?

2. How would you describe Brian Wood's commitment to his wife? Are you ready to make a sacrifice like that for your wife or future spouse?

3. In what practical way can you be your wife's savior today? Or, if you're single, how can you prepare yourself to be a kingdom husband?

PRAYER

God, show me how to love my wife (or future wife) as sacrificially as You love Your church. And in doing so, please make me more like Jesus. Amen.

81

A Kingdom Man Cherishes His Wife

You are the sunshine of my life.
That's why I'll always stay around.
—Stevie Wonder, "You Are the Sunshine of My Life"

The lyrics to the pop songs we listened to growing up express strong opinions about love and devotion, but even the best lyrics come up short. They'd have us scaling mountains, storming castles, or impulsively catching a red-eye flight to prove our affection. Conventional wisdom suggests roses to encourage romance. Or dinner by candlelight. But a wife needs much more than flowers or one-time grand gestures to feel cherished by her husband; she needs to be sanctified and satisfied (Ephesians 5:25–30).

Sanctification involves setting your wife apart and creating a safe place for her to bloom into God's kingdom woman. That's an ongoing process requiring patience, sensitivity, and spiritual mentoring . . . from you. When you said, "I do," you also married her history. If she hasn't known security in the home of a kingdom man before, she may be hesitant to submit. Gentle sanctification will bathe her in the freedom to experience all God has for her.

In addition, we need to *satisfy* our wives emotionally, spiritually, and yes, physically. But hold on, Romeo. Those aren't three separate elevators to her heart. They're connected. For a woman to respond intimately, she must first respond with her soul. Forget about Victoria's Secret. Here's God's secret: The only way to satisfy your wife is by creating spiritual oneness.

APPLICATION

1. How does your wife know that you cherish her? If you're single, are there any good husbands that you know? What do they do to cherish their wives?

2. What song lyrics have influenced your sense of what a woman needs?

3. What can you do or say to sanctify your wife today? Or, if you're single, what can you do to prepare yourself to be a good husband?

PRAYER

Father, please give me understanding so that I might satisfy my wife's (or future wife's) emotional, spiritual, and physical needs on her terms, not mine. Amen.

82

A Kingdom Man Is Focused on the Right Thing

When I shot the shot, everything felt fine.
—Matt Emmons, to reporters at the 2004 Olympic Games

Matt Emmons exhaled deeply. *Just stay calm,* he thought. *One more shot and the gold medal is mine.* Leading by three points in the 2004 Summer Olympics three-position rifle event, Emmons knew his final shot only needed to get near the bull's-eye to assure victory. He focused on the target fifty meters away and pulled the trigger.

Pop! His shot hit just outside the center circle. The gold medal was his . . . or was it? The scoreboard didn't register any points. Emmons saw the tournament officials gathered. He figured there had been a scoring malfunction, but he figured wrong. Emmons had taken his final shot in lane two, but hit the target in lane *three.* By cross-firing on his final shot, he earned zero points and dropped from first to eighth. Emmons's aim was perfect and would've scored him enough points to win gold; however, he'd focused on the wrong target.[1]

The problem that we face in the church today is not insincerity; it is that the church is focusing on the wrong assignment. By misunderstanding the nature and purpose of God's kingdom, we have marginalized the church's authority and influence both within its walls and outside them.

The nature of God's kingdom on earth is a biblical mandate to be relevant to the spiritual and sociological needs in today's society. The church does not exist for programs, projects, preaching, and buildings; rather, it exists as the primary vehicle for preparing believers to display God's glory, impact the culture, restore lives, and advance the kingdom.

APPLICATION

1. What target are you focused on?

2. How could you develop better aim and display more of God's glory?

3. What can you do in your church to impact the culture?

PRAYER

Jesus, help me to focus on the right target. May my efforts be aimed at You and Your kingdom. Amen.

83

A Kingdom Man Is
Part of Something
Bigger Than Himself

For even as the body is one and yet has
many members, and all the members
of the body, though they are many,
are one body, so also is Christ.
—1 Corinthians 12:12

Over the last hundred years, the number of Christians around the world has nearly quadrupled. In 1910, six hundred million people claimed to follow Christ. In 2010, the number had topped two billion! A study of more than two hundred countries found that one out of every three people on the planet is a Christian. And unlike in 1910 when Europeans and Americans comprised 93 percent of the Christian population, now Christ has truly gone global. Sub-Saharan Africa and the Asia-Pacific region have seen the greatest percentage of increase in people giving their lives to Christ.[1]

When it comes to God's family, you are not an only

child. Jesus taught the disciples to pray, "*Our* Father who is in heaven" (Matthew 6:9), not "*My* Father who is in heaven." As a follower of Jesus, you are part of something larger than yourself. When you involve yourself in the community of believers, you get more out of your experience with God and His blessings in your life.

Just as Satan seeks to break up the family in an effort to destroy the future, he also wants to break up the community of believers because he knows that an anemic church will never experience the presence of God. God is a God of unity, and where there is disunity and division, His Spirit is not free to dwell.

APPLICATION

1. How does it feel knowing that so many people share your beliefs?

2. Where do you see disunity in the church today?

3. How can you help build unity in your community of believers?

PRAYER

Father, help me to see beyond myself. Make me a builder of unity within Your kingdom. Amen.

84

A Kingdom Man Is an Example to His Family

Be imitators of me, just as I also am of Christ.
—1 Corinthians 11:1

Hall of Fame wide receiver Jerry Rice holds just about every meaningful receiving record in the NFL. He's first in career receiving touchdowns, first in receptions, first in all-time receiving yards.[1] Teammates and coaches could always rely on him to show up on Sunday.

"The thing that made him most special was that he had the God-given abilities and he went beyond those abilities because of the way that he worked and his dedication to perfecting his game," former San Francisco 49ers coach George Seifert said. "The way he interacted with the players and coaches—he was somebody that took to coaching and wanted to be the best."[2]

Rice was an example to his teammates in his preparation and dedication. His off-season workouts with running back Roger Craig were legendary, often inspiring fellow teammates to work harder to be the best they could be.[3]

My father wanted me to be the best I could be, and he knew that meant showing up on Sunday. As a child growing up under his leadership, I remember that I would practically need to be hospitalized to get out of going to church on Sunday. Even though I wasn't at the point in my own spiritual development to benefit from the service as much as my father, his consistency in embracing the role of the church in his life set the example for doing so in my own life as I grew older. In fact, by the time I was in high school, my dad's biblical worldview had become my own.

APPLICATION

1. What example are you setting for your family?

2. How are you following Christ's example?

3. How can you make church and growing in your faith more of a priority?

PRAYER

God, I want my example to draw my family and the people around me closer to You. Help me be consistent in my walk. Amen.

85

A Kingdom Man Is Rooted with Other Believers

Iron sharpens iron, so one man sharpens another.
—Proverbs 27:17

Scientists say the largest living thing on earth is a single male quaking aspen colony in south-central Utah. Nicknamed *Pando,* the Latin word for "I spread," these trees cover more than 100 acres and weigh in excess of thirteen million pounds. But that's not the amazing thing. What's more amazing is that *Pando* began as a *single* tree. Quaking aspens spread through their roots, so all 47,000 trees in this colony are connected by an intricate, underground root system. The roots shoot out, young trees sprout through the soil, and eventually grow into mature trees.[1]

It's the same way with discipleship. Discipleship is a developmental process of the local church that brings Christians from spiritual infancy to spiritual maturity. Through discipleship, Christian men will be better connected and rooted to God.

When a man faces obstacles and challenges in his quest

to live as a kingdom man, the support system for facing those obstacles victoriously that God has placed on earth is the local church. Life is not to be lived as a lone ranger. That would be similar to putting the starting quarterback on the line at the beginning of the football game and facing him off against eleven other players—alone—while telling him to overcome that obstacle. Oneness in the body of Christ—whether racially, generationally, or within relationships among men—is a requirement to advance the kingdom simply because of the nature of the body.

APPLICATION

1. What are some benefits of being connected other men?

2. Why do you think men tend to act like lone rangers?

3. Do you have a discipleship group or accountability partner? If not, what can you do today to find one? If you have one, what can you do to make it a deeper relationship?

PRAYER

Lord, I know I'm stronger when I'm connected to others and to You. Help me support other men in Your body. Amen.

86

A Kingdom Man Lives His Faith Publicly

My encouragement is to be bold wherever and whenever. It's pretty amazing to see what God's been able to do just because I was obedient and started to take those little steps to step out.

—Kurt Warner, interview with *Focus on the Family Breakaway* magazine editor Jesse Florea, 2001

Kurt Warner came out of nowhere to shock the NFL in 1999. Undrafted out of college, Warner played in the Arena Football League from 1995–1997. The St. Louis Rams signed him as their third-string quarterback in 1998. When the Rams starting quarterback got injured in 1999, Warner became the starter. In his first four games, Warner threw fourteen touchdown passes—two more than the Rams had completed in the entire 1998 season![1]

When reporters asked about the secret to his success, Warner answered, "It's my faith in Jesus Christ."[2]

He led the Rams to a victory in Super Bowl XXXIV. Warner earned MVP honors, making him just the seventh player in football history to take home the league and Super Bowl MVP awards in the same year.[3]

During Warner's Arena League days, he told his wife that his faith was between him and God—nobody else needed to know. But he became convicted about keeping Jesus a secret and decided to begin sharing his faith. Soon his opportunities to serve Christ grew immeasurably.[4]

This is not a time for secret-agent Christians or covert Jesus operatives. We need kingdom men who will step up and change the world. No one pays for a ticket to a football game just to watch the huddle. You have to break the huddle and show what you can do. Dare to go public.

APPLICATION

1. How have you shown your faith in Christ lately?

2. Second Corinthians 5:20 says kingdom men are "ambassadors for Christ." How should you act as Christ's ambassador?

3. What hindrances are keeping you from being more public with your faith?

PRAYER

Lord, help me break the huddle and go public for You. Amen.

87

A Kingdom Man
Makes an Impact

A life is not important, except in the
impact it has on other lives.
—Jackie Robinson, *I Never Had It Made*

When Jim Hosier laces up his bowling shoes, he almost immediately goes on a roll—literally. No person in the history of the sport has bowled more perfect games. To score a perfect 300, you must roll twelve consecutive strikes. That sounds nearly impossible to a novice bowler. Hosier is no novice. He has competed in three to five bowling leagues for most of his life and racked up an amazing 133 perfect games in sanctioned play.[1]

When some men step into a bowling alley, they try to look the part of a seasoned bowler like Hosier. They wear certain clothes and bowl with an elite ball. (Hosier owns sixteen balls, but he usually carries only four with him.[2]) Yet the thing I find amusing is that no matter how great a man looks while bowling, if his ball goes in the gutter, he's a failure. The goal of bowling is knocking down pins, not looking the part of a bowler.

We have a lot of fancy churches in our country with a lot of fancy-looking men attending them. But the true test of a church—and of a man—is not how good it looks, but the kind of impact it makes in the community. If we are going to have restored communities, God's men have to start being real men rather than simply trying to look like men on the outside.

APPLICATION

1. What is more pressure: trying to bowl a perfect game or to make an impact for God?

2. Would you rather look good or do good? Why?

3. What are the characteristics of a *real* man?

PRAYER

Jesus, I don't want to just look like a Christian, I want to act like one. Help me to make an impact for You. Amen.

A Kingdom Man Loves Well

You can give without loving, but you
cannot love without giving.
—John Wooden, *Wooden: A Lifetime*
of Observations and Reflections

John Wooden led the UCLA men's basketball team to
ten NCAA championships in twelve years. During one
stretch, his Bruins won eighty-eight games in a row.[1] Both
are coaching records that may never be broken.

Wooden was a master of details and blending talent.
He taught his players the minutiae, like how to put on
their socks, and the significant, like how to play defense
and work as team. More than twenty years after retiring
from coaching, Wooden looked back at his career and
said the two most important things to his success were
love and balance.[2] Wooden loved his players and his players loved him. Kareem Abdul-Jabbar and Bill Walton still
gush about their college coach.[3] Wooden called love "the
most important thing there is."[4] Love is not soft. It is not
incompatible with being a man; instead it is essential.

Men, leading well involves loving well. It involves aligning yourself under God in such a way that you place the best interests of those within your realm as a priority in your life. Putting the best interest of others above your own means recognizing God's headship in fulfilling your own and modeling yourself after the greatest leader of all—God himself. What has negatively impacted our society so much is the number of men, particularly men within Christian circles, who attempt to bully those around them through claiming the title of "head" without exercising the responsibilities that come with that title such as leading, providing, and loving.

APPLICATION

1. Who were the best leaders in your life? What made them good leaders?

2. Does love make you weak? Why or why not?

3. What leadership qualities of Jesus do you want to emulate?

PRAYER

Jesus, I want to love others, especially those I lead, in the same way that You love me. Amen.

A Kingdom Man Strengthens Those in Need

*Truly I say to you, to the extent that you did
it to one of these brothers of Mine, even
the least of them, you did it to Me.*
—Matthew 25:40

Since its inception in 2000, the Bill and Melinda Gates Foundation has donated more than $26.1 billion to charity.[1] David Timothy isn't nearly as well-known as the Gates—except to the homeless in the Dallas area. In August 2003, Timothy took an old Ford van and started the SoupMobile. That year, Timothy (aka the SoupMan) drove around and served 5,000 meals. Today, he serves more than 200,000 meals a year, and he's opened Soup-Mobile Village Homes to provide shelter to the homeless.[2]

The reason Timothy serves is simple. Two thousand years ago, Jesus said, "Feed My sheep" (John 21:17, HCSB). Timothy didn't always have a heart for the homeless. He was a successful businessman who ate at fine restaurants. "God took me from a guy who had a lot of *I*'s in his life—

I this, I that," Timothy says. "From a selfish, self-centered guy to somebody who'd be willing to serve."[3]

God's heart is found in strengthening those in need. If we know God, then we ought to be about the things He is about—which always includes helping others. In helping those in need, we introduce a system, one created by God, that shows the world what happens when a society follows God as a Ruler. By reaching out in the name of Jesus Christ, we address the underlying spiritual issues—not just the temporary physical issues—and can enact true life change.

APPLICATION

1. Where is the greatest need in your community?

2. How can you get involved in a ministry that addresses that need?

3. James 1:27 tells us to "look after widows and orphans in their distress" (HCSB). What do you think that means for you today?

PRAYER

Lord, You came to help the needy. Give me a heart like Yours and the opportunity to make a difference. Amen.

A Kingdom Man
Passes the Baton

Leadership is more like a baton than a trophy.
You keep a trophy, but you hand off a baton. In
a race, if you don't hand off the baton, you lose.

—Bruce Miller, coauthor of *The Leadership Baton*

Few sporting events can match the excitement of the 4 x 100 relay. Speeds surpass twenty-three miles per hour[1] as four sprinters fly around the track, passing a baton to see who can make it to the finish line first. Since the inception of the 4 x 100 relay, the United States men's and women's teams combined have claimed Olympic gold twenty-five times. The next closest nation, Jamaica, has earned just three golds in the event.[2]

At the 2008 Summer Games, the United States entered with two powerful relay teams. But on a rainy night in Beijing, both the men's and women's 4 x 100 teams dropped their batons in the semifinals. In both cases, the missed exchange came when the US team was ahead. And in both cases, the US team was disqualified.[3]

We're living in a generation where men don't know how to pass the baton of blessing. In biblical times, men lived for the blessing. A blessing involved divine destiny, significance, authority, and a productive future. The blessing was always tied not merely to what you were, but also to what you were destined to become. This generation of boys has never been blessed because there is a generation of men that has never been blessed. So there's nothing to pass down. It's like running a relay race with no baton.

Kingdom men, man up. Turn your hearts toward your children. Learn the importance of the blessing. Make sure God's covenant promise is passed down to future generations.

Application

1. What position in your family's relay are you? Front runner? Anchor? Middle?

2. Why do you think the blessing is important?

3. How are you passing the baton in your life?

Prayer

God, I want to pass down Your blessing. Help me hand over my baton without dropping it. Amen.

Notes

Devo 1

1. International Movie Database (IMDb.com), *Indiana Jones and the Last Crusade*, Quotes, http://www.imdb.com/title /tt0097576/trivia?tab=qt&ref_=tt_trv_qu.

2. International Movie Database (IMDb.com), *Indiana Jones and the Last Crusade*, Plot Summary, http://www.imdb.com /title/tt0097576/plotsummary.

Devo 3

1. Gary Smith, "Remember His Name," Sports Illustrated, September 5, 2006, http://sportsillustrated.cnn.com/2006 /magazine/09/05/tillman0911/2.html.

Devo 4

1. Peter King, "Lack of Communication Ultimately Led to Embarrassing Monday Gaffe," *Sports Illustrated*, September 25, 2012, http://sportsillustrated.cnn.com/2012/writers /peter_king/09/25/replacement-referees-packers-seahawks /index.html#ixzz2RMG97Ksd.

Devo 5

1. Sources for "Miracle on the Hudson," are as follows: USAirways.com, "US Airways flight 1549 transcript," http://www.usairways.com/en-US/aboutus/pressroom /1549_transcript.html; "Captain Chesley B. Sullenberger III," http://www.usairways.com/en-US/aboutus/pressroom

/Sullenbergerbio.html; CBS News.com, "Flight 1549: A
Routine Takeoff Turns Ugly," July 6, 2009, http://www
.cbsnews.com/stories/2009/02/08/60minutes/ main47835
80.shtml; "Flight 1549: Saving 155 Souls In Minutes," July
6, 2009, http://www.cbsnews.com/stories/2009/02/08
/60minutes/main4783586.shtml; Fox News.com,
"Surveillance Video Released of US Airways Plane Landing
in Hudson River," January 17, 2009, http://www.fox
news.com/story/0,2933,480412,00.html; Kerry Burke,
Pete Donohue, and Corky Siemasko, NYDailyNews.com,
"US Airways airplane crashes in Hudson River—Hero
pilot Chesley Sullenberger III saves all aboard," January 15,
2009, http://articles.nydailynews.com/2009-01-15/news
/17914076_1_hero-pilot-air-force-fighter-crash-landed;
Federal Aviation Administration, "INFORMATION: Full
Transcript Aircraft Accident, AWE1549 New York, NY,
January 15, 2009," http://www.faa.gov/data_research
/accident_incident/1549/media/CD.pdf.

Devo 6

1. Story adapted from Tony Evans, *No More Excuses* (Wheaton,
   IL: Crossway, 1996), 167.

Devo 7

1. Adapted from Tony Evans, *Tony Evans' Book of Illustrations*
   (Chicago: Moody, 2009), 178; and Charles Siebert, "An
   Elephant Crackup?" *New York Times Magazine*, October 8,
   2006, http://www.nytimes.com/2006/10/08/magazine
   /08elephant.html?pagewanted=all&_r=0.

2. National Fatherhood Initiative, "The Father Factor," http://
www.fatherhood.org/media/consequences-of-father-absence
-statistics; and Sara McLanahan, "Father Absence and the
Welfare of Children," Network on the Family and the
Economy, accessed May 9, 2013, http://apps.olin.wustl
.edu/macarthur/working%20papers/wp-mclanahan2
.htm.

Devo 10

1. Story adapted from Tony Evans, *No More Excuses* (Wheaton,
IL: Crossway, 1996), xi.

Devo 11

1. Michael Jordan, "Michael Jordan's Basketball Hall of Fame
Enshrinement Speech," 18:20–19:00 minutes, http://www
.youtube.com/watch?v=XLzBMGXfK4c.

Devo 13

1. Ian Thomsen, "My Sportsman: Dirk Nowitzki," *Sports
Illustrated*, December 2, 2011, http://sportsillustrated.cnn
.com/2011/magazine/sportsman/11/25/thomsen.nowitzki
/index.html.
2. Tom Ziller, *SB Nation*, June 12, 2011, http://www.sb
nation.com/nba/2011/6/12/2220926/dirk-nowitzki-nba
-finals-mvp-2011-dallas-mavericks-miami-heat.

Devo 14

1. Jim Collins, "The Misguided Mix-up of Celebrity and
Leadership," Conference Board Annual Report, Annual

Feature Essay, September/October 2001, http://www.jim
collins.com/article_topics/articles/the-misguided-mixup
.html.

Devo 17

1. Sources for information about Ray Guy include Mark
   Heisler, "After 14 Lofty Seasons, Raiders' Ray Guy
   Retires: Nagging Injuries and Declining Punting
   Average Force Him to Make Decision," *Los Angeles
   Times*, June 3, 1987, http://articles.latimes.com/1987
   -06-03/sports/sp-2483_1_ray-guy; Les Carpenter,
   "Legendary Raiders Punter Ray Guy Frustrated but
   Resigned That He's Not in Hall of Fame," *Yahoo! Sports*,
   November 14, 2012, http://sports.yahoo.com/news
   /nfl--legendary-punter-ray-guy-frustrated--but-resigned
   -that-he-s-not-in-hall-of-fame.html; and Zac Wassink,
   "Best punters in NFL history," *Yahoo! Contributor
   Network*, Sept 27, 2010, http://sports.yahoo.com/nfl
   /news?slug=ac-6830106.

Devo 20

1. "Top Execs Who Started at the Bottom: Wally Amos,"
   CNBC, http://www.cnbc.com/id/43896634/page/4; Dana
   Canedy, "A Famous Cookie and a Face to Match; How
   Wally Amos Got His Hand and His Name Back in the
   Game," *New York Times*, July 3, 1999, http://www.nytimes
   .com/1999/07/03/business/famous-cookie-face-match
   -wally-amos-got-his-hand-his-name-back-game.html?page
   wanted=all&src=pm.

Devo 21

1. International Movie Database (IMDb), *The Matrix,* http:// www.imdb.com/title/tt0133093/ and quoted in *The Matrix,* "Blue Pill or Red Pill—The Matrix (2/9) Movie CLIP (1999) HD," YouTube, http://www.youtube.com /watch?v=zE7PKRjrid4.

Devo 22

1. Pro Football Hall of Fame, "National Football League Championship Game Play by Play, December 28, 1958," http://www.profootballhof.com/assets/history /58_Championship_PxP.pdf.
2. Frank Gifford and Peter Richmond, *The Glory Game* (New York: Harper Collins, 2008), front flap copy.
3. "NFL's All-Decade Team of the 1950s," Pro Football Hall of Fame, http://www.profootballhof.com/story /2010/1/16/nfls-all-decade-team-of-the-1950s/.
4. "Lenny Moore," Pro Football Hall of Fame, http:// www.profootballhof.com/hof/member.aspx?PLAYER _ID=155.

Devo 23

1. International Movie Database (IMDb), *Wall Street,* "Quotes," http://www.imdb.com/title/tt0094291/trivia ?tab=qt&ref_=tt_trv_qu.

Devo 25

1. Bio.True Story, "Theodore Roosevelt. Biography," http:// www.biography.com/people/theodore-roosevelt-9463424.

Devo 26

1. National Vital Statistics Reports, Vol. 59, No. 1, December 8, 2010, http://www.cdc.gov/nchs/data/nvsr/nvsr59/nvsr59_01_tables.pdf#tableI04.

Devo 28

1. Douglas W. Philips, *The Birkenhead Drill* (San Antonio, TX: The Vision Forum, 2001), 24, 37, 39, 40, 76; ElectronicScotland.com, "74th Highlanders: 1846–1853," http://www.electricscotland.com/history/scotreg/74th-2.htm; University of Wolverhampton, "Shared Heritage: Management of British Warship Wrecks Overseas," July 8, 2008, http://www.english-heritage.org.uk/publications/management-of-british-warship-wrecks-overseas/shared-heritage-management-of-british-warship-wrecks-overseas.pdf and The Queen's Royal Surreys Regimental Association, "The Birkenhead Disaster 26th February, 1852," http://www.queensroyalsurreys.org.uk/1661to1966/birkenhead/birkenhead.html.

Devo 33

1. Tim MacMahon, "Rick Carlisle's best work? Nothing tops title run," ESPN, April 1, 2013, http://espn.go.com/blog/dallas/mavericks/post/_/id/4695380/rick-carlisles-best-work-nothing-can-top-11-title-run; http://bleacherreport.com/articles/1349527-where-does-dallas-mavericks-rick-carlisle-rank-among-nbas-best-coaches

2. All men are to be under the authority of the church leadership. A married woman is under the authority

of her husband who in turn is under the authority of the church. A single woman is to be under the spiritual covering of the church because she has no husband, unless she is still living under the authority of her father (1 Corinthians 7).

Devo 35

1. Kathryn Hatter "Facts on Bamboo Plants," eHow, http://www.ehow.com/about_5047713_bamboo-plants.html.

Devo 39

1. C. S. Lewis, *The Lion, the Witch and the Wardrobe*, (New York: HarperCollins, 1950), 164.

Devo 41

1. Frances Hodgson Burnett, *The Secret Garden* (New York: Frederick A. Stokes, 1911), 282.

Devo 42

1. "Auburn fires Gene Chizik," ESPN, Nov. 25, 2012, http://espn.go.com/college-football/story/_/id/8674097/gene-chizik-fired-auburn-tigers; Gary Klein, "Auburn defeats Oregon, 22-19, to win BCS national championship game," *Los Angeles Times*, Jan 10, 2011, http://articles.latimes.com/2011/jan/10/sports/la-sp-bcs-championship-live11; and "Auburn claims SEC's fifth straight national title by dropping Oregon on late field goal," ESPN, http://scores.espn.go.com/ncf/recap?gameId=310102483.

Devo 44

1. Nick Vujicic, quoted in promotional "Book Description" copy for *Life Without Limits* by Nick Vujicic., http://www.amazon.com/Life-Without-Limits -Inspiration-Ridiculously/dp/0307589749, accessed April 17, 2013.

Devo 45

1. Brian Kamenetzky, "Top 10 Lakers Playoff Moments: Magic Jumps Center," ESPN LA, May 26, 1980, http:// espn.go.com/blog/los-angeles/lakers/post/_/id/7473/top -10-lakers-playoff-moments-magic-jumps-center and Rick Weinberg, "63: Magic Moves to Center, Beats Sixers for Title," ESPN, http://sports.espn.go.com/espn/espn25 /story?page=moments/63.

Devo 47

1. C. S. Lewis, *The Fellowship of the Ring*, (New York: Houghton Mifflin, 2004), chapter 2.

Devo 49

1. USAHockey.com, "U.S. Hockey Hall of Fame: The 1980 U.S. Olympic Team," http://www.usahockey .com/ushhof/default.aspx?NAV=AF_01&id=289 718; and Sports Illustrated, "10 Interesting Facts You May Not Know about 1980 Miracle on Ice," sports illustrated.cnn.com/2010/writers/joe_posnanski/02 /22./index.html.

Devo 50

1. Ryan Bradley and Ed Stafford, "Adventurers of the Year 2010: The Explorer: Ed Stafford," *National Geographic*, http://adventure.nationalgeographic.com/adventure /adventurers-of-the-year/ed-stafford-2010/; and Walking the Amazon, accessed April 29, 2013, http://www .walkingtheamazon.com/faq.

Devo 51

1. Brian Schmitz, "Bob Kurland Is the Grand-daddy of the Dunk," *Orlando Sentinel,* February 19, 2012, http:// articles.orlandosentinel.com/2012-02-19/sports/os-bob -kurland-dunk-0219-20120219_1_dunk-blake-griffin -nba-all-star; and Basketball Hall of Fame, "Hall of Famers: Robert A. "Bob" Kurland," accessed May 13, 2012, http://www.hoophall.com/hall-of-famers/tag/robert -a-bob-kurland.

Devo 52

1. Austin Murphy, "The Maddest 2 Minutes in Sports," *Sports Illustrated*, February 4, 2013, http://sports illustrated.cnn.com/vault/article/magazine/MAG1206 790/index.htm.

Devo 54

1. Adapted from Tony Evans, *Tony Evans' Book of Illustrations* (Chicago: Moody, 2009), 315.

Devo 55

1. 'Three Years Six Months—the Moment Married Partners
   Start Taking Each Other for Granted," *The Telegraph*,
   February 8, 2013, http://www.telegraph.co.uk/news
   /uknews/9857659/Three-years-six-months-the-moment
   -married-partners-start-taking-each-other-for-granted
   .html.

Devo 59

1. ESPN NFL, "Game HQ: Scores for Jan 22, 2012," http://
   scores.espn.go.com/nfl/recap?gameId=320122025 and Josh
   Dubow, "San Franciso 49ers Miss Chance at Super Bowl
   after Kyle Williams Fumble," *Huffington Post*, January 22,
   2012, http://www.huffingtonpost.com/2012/01/23
   /san-francisco-49ers-kyle-williams-fumble-lose-video_n_12
   23453.html.

Devo 61

1. Andrew Marchand, "Russell Martin: I Hate the Red Sox,"
   ESPN New York, September 24, 2011, http://espn.go
   .com/new-york/mlb/story/_/id/7005688/new-york
   -yankees-russell-martin-hate-boston-red-sox.

Devo 63

1. Rick Weinberg, "89: Rulon Gardner Stops Invincible
   Karelin," ESPN25, accessed May 1, 2013, http://sports
   .espn.go.com/espn/espn25/story?page=moments/89

Devo 64

1. Rick Weinbert, "Montana Hits Clark to Win NFC Championship," ESPN25, accessed May 1, 2013, http://sports.espn.go.com/espn/espn25/story?page=moments/14; and "The Catch," You Tube, uploaded January 18, 2008, originally aired on CBS, January 10, 1982, http://www.youtube.com/watch?v=tunyz0WWLSI.

Devo 66

1. About.com: Inventors, "The History of the Automobile: The Internal Combustion Engine and the Early Gas-Powered Cars," accessed May 1, 2013, http://inventors.about.com/library/weekly/aacarsgasa.htm; and Richard Slawsky, "The History of Windshields," http://www.ehow.com/about_5080079_history-windshields.html.

Devo 67

1. Bible History Online, "Ancient Wine Press," accessed May 1, 2013, http://www.bible-history.com/sketches/ancient/wine-press.html.
2. *Strong's Concordance,* s.v. "Hebrew 1869 *darak,*" http://biblesuite.com/hebrew/1869.htm.

Devo 68

1. Matt Stevens, "Woman finds $23-million Lotto ticket left in car for months," *Los Angeles Times* (blog), November 1,

2012, http://latimesblogs.latimes.com/lanow/2012/11
/23-million-lotto-ticket-left-in-glove-compartment-for
-months-.html.

Devo 69

1. Wikipedia, s.v. "2005–6 George Mason Patriots men's
   basketball team," http://en.wikipedia.org/wiki/2005%
   E2%80%9306_George_Mason_Patriots_men%27s
   _basketball_team.

Devo 70

1. Billy Graham, "Billy Graham's *My Answer*," August 16,
   2012, http://www.billygraham.org/articlepage.asp?articleid
   =8858.

Devo 71

1. Orville and Wilbur Wright, "The Wright Brothers
   Aeroplane," *Century Magazine*, September 1908, http://
   libraries.wright.edu/special/wright_brothers/info_packet
   /century_magazine.pdf.

Devo 72

1. Caitlin A. Johnson, "Cutting Through Advertising
   Clutter," CBSNews.com, 2/11/09, http://www.cbsnews
   .com/8301-3445_162-2015684.html.

Devo 74

1. Kessler R. C., Chiu W. T., Demler O., Walters E.E., "Prevalence, Severity, and Comorbidity of Twelve-month DSM-IV Disorders in the National Comorbidity Survey Replication (NCS-R)," *Archives of General Psychiatry,* June 2005, 62(6):617–27 cited in National Institute of Mental Health (nimh.nih.gov), "Anxiety Disorders: Phobias," http://www.nimh.nih.gov/health/publications/anxiety-disorders/specific-phobias.shtml.

2. *Strong's Concordance,* s.v. "Hebrew 3373 *yare,*" http://biblesuite.com/hebrew/3373.htm.

Devo 76

1. Adapted from Tony Evans, *Tony Evans' Book of Illustrations* (Chicago: Moody, 2009), 106.

Devo 77

1. Adriana Camarena, "New Generation Meets Iconic Bicycle Messenger," Nowtopian (blog), September 25, 2009, http://www.nowtopians.com/work-and-the-economy/new-generation-meets-iconic-bicycle-messenger.

Devo 78

1. SportingNews NBA, "Dikembe Mutombo Enjoys Return to Shot-Blocking Spotlight," February 26, 2013, http://aol.sportingnews.com/nba/story/2013-02-26/dikembe-mutombo-geico-tv-ad-not-in-my-house-blocked-shots;

and NBA.com, "Dikembe Mutombo," http://www.nba
.com/playerfile/dikembe_mutombo/.

2. YouTube, "Geico commercial: Happier Than Dikembe
   Mutombo Blocking a Shot," posted March 5, 2013,
   accessed May 1, 2013, http://www.youtube.com/watch
   ?v=dU6SXjhIOho.

Devo 79

1. Heritage History, s.v. "Hernando Cortez," accessed May 1,
   2013, http://www.heritage-history.com/www/heritage.php
   ?Dir=characters&FileName=cortez.php.

Devo 80

1. Allie Pruitt, "Brian Wood," *Weekly World News*, September
   17, 2010, http://weeklyworldnews.com/headlines/22254
   /brian-wood/.

Devo 82

1. Steve Rivera, "Emmons Loses Gold Medal after Aiming
   at Wrong Target," *USA Today*, August 22, 2004, http://
   usatoday30.usatoday.com/sports/olympics/athens/skill
   /2004-08-22-shooting-emmons_x.htm.

Devo 83

1. The Pew Forum on Religious and Public Life, "Global
   Christianity: A Report on the Size and Distribution of the
   World's Christian Population," December 19, 2011, http://
   www.pewforum.org/Christian/Global-Christianity-exec.aspx.

Devo 84

1. Pro-Football-Reference.com, "Jerry Rice," accessed April 28, 2013, http://www.pro-football-reference.com/players/R /RiceJe00.htm; and Jerry Rice, "Records and Accomplishments," accessed April 28, 2013, http://www.jerryrice.net /JerryRice/accompli.htm.
2. Taylor Price, "Teammates, Coaches Reflect on Rice," San Francisco 49ers (blog), February 6, 2010, http://blog.49ers .com/2010/02/06/teammates-coaches-reflect-on-rice/.
3. Ibid.

Devo 85

1. Michael C. Grant, "The Trembling Giant," *Discover Magazine*, October 1, 1993, http://discovermagazine. com/1993/oct/thetremblinggian285#.UXfy1HF3_V0; and *Wikipedia*, s.v. "Pando," http://en.wikipedia.org/wiki /Pando_%28tree%29.

Devo 86

1. Michael Silver, "Holy Smokes," October 18, 1999, *SI Vault*, http://sportsillustrated.cnn.com/vault/article /magazine/MAG1017358/.
2. Ibid.
3. Stuart Miller, "Most Valuable Disconnect: Regular Season and Super Bowl," *New York Times* (nytimes .com), December 19, 2009, "http://www.nytimes .com/2009/12/20/sports/football/20score.html?_r =1&.

4. Kurt Warner in interview with *Focus on the Family Breakaway* magazine editor Jesse Florea, August 2001.

Devo 87

1. Chuck Pezzano, "Wayne's Perfect Bowler," June 11, 2012, *NorthJersey.com*, http://www.northjersey.com/sports/1583 95195_Wayne_s_perfect_bowler.html.
2. Ibid.

Devo 88

1. Bob Bensch, "John Wooden, Winner of 10 NCAA Titles, Dies at Age 99," Bloomberg, June 4, 2010, http://www .bloomberg.com/news/2010-06-05/john-wooden-winner -of-10-ncaa-basketball-titles-at-ucla-dies-at-age-99.html.
2. Terry Starbucker (blog), "Leadership—What's Love Got to Do with It?" November 29, 2009, http://www.terry starbucker.com/2009/11/29/leadership-whats-love-got -to-do-with-it/.
3. Dick Weiss, "To Kareem Abdul-Jabbar and Bill Walton, UCLA's John Wooden Was More Than a Coach," *Daily News*, June 5, 2010, http://www.nydailynews.com/sports /college/kareem-abdul-jabbar-bill-walton-ucla-john -wooden-coach-article-1.179134.
4. See note 2.

Devo 89

1. The Bill and Melinda Gates Foundation, "Who We Are: Foundation Fact Sheet," accessed April 27, 2013,

  http://www.gatesfoundation.org/Who-We-Are/General
  -Information/Foundation-Factsheet.

2. SoupMobile, "History," accessed April 27, 2013, http://
   www.soupmobile.org/about-us/history.

3. David Timothy, "What Jesus Taught the SoupMan," You
   Tube, http://www.youtube.com/watch?v=IkccMlC3h9E.

Devo 90

1. Planet Science, "How Fast Is Usain Bolt?" accessed, April
   28, 2013, http://www.planet-science.com/categories/over
   -11s/human-body/2012/06/how-fast-is-usain-bolt.aspx.

2. *Wikipedia*, s.v. "4 x 100 metres relay," accessed April 27,
   2013, http://en.wikipedia.org/wiki/4_×_100_metres_relay.

3. Dick Patrick, "Baton Drops Mar U.S. Efforts in Both
   4 x 100 Relays," *USA Today,* August 22, 2008, http://
   usatoday30.usatoday.com/sports/olympics/beijing/track
   /2008-08-21-sprintrelays_N.htm.